# **PIANO** BURNING

## and Other

## Fighter Pilot Traditions

– Rob Burgon –

Cover design: Rob Burgon, typography by Alex Kolody

Published by Slipstream Publishing, Salt Lake City, Utah.

ISBN: 0-9984132-1-6

ISBN-13: 978-0-9984132-1-1

This book is dedicated to my son, and fighter pilot at heart, Everett. It is also dedicated to all the courageous members — past, present, and future — of the 8th Fighter Squadron "Black Sheep." Once a Sheep... ALWAYS A SHEEP!

# Table of Contents

# Preface

"Chief, am I clear to start the APU?" I asked my lead maintainer over the intercom. From my vantage point in the cockpit of the Air Dominance fighter, I couldn't see the exhaust vent of the Auxiliary Power Unit (APU) located just aft of the left diamond-shaped air intake. If someone was standing near it when I started the jet, the heat from the exhaust would cook them.

"All clear, sir!" said the Crew Chief.

My heart racing, I pushed the APU switch forward and held it until I saw the green *APU Run* light illuminate. There was a brief delay, followed by a loud hissing sound as compressed air from an onboard storage bottle shot through the mini turbine engine of the APU. With the flick of a switch, I lowered the large bubble canopy of the F-22.

No fighter pilot ever forgets the first time he closes the canopy of a jet with no one else in the aircraft.

There is a quiet, ethereal feeling in the cockpit of a single-seat fighter as you seemingly remove yourself from the rest of the world. My experience on this day was no exception. The euphoria I felt as the gold-tinted canopy slowly closed, encapsulating me alone for the first time in the $160-million fighter plane, will stay with me forever.

I was practically choking on the adrenaline coursing through my body. I had to consciously keep my legs from doing an impression of Elvis Presley as I stood on the brakes in preparation for starting the engines. The oxygen mask dangling from the left side of my helmet was pushed away by the wide grin on my face as, one-by-one, I lifted the throttles out of *cut-off* into the *idle* position. Each engine gave a low growl as the turbines of the powerful Pratt and Whitney F119s roared to life.

There are no words to describe the feeling of my first flight in the Lockheed/Martin F-22 Raptor. I can describe what happened on the sortie, but unless you are the one with 70,000 pounds of thrust at your fingertips, you can only imagine what it feels like to suck up the landing gear and point the aircraft's nose straight up. It's hard not to let out a cheer when you roll inverted to bring the nose back down to the horizon at level-off. You feel like King Kong at 18,000 feet over the departure end of the runway.

I flew alone that day, as I did every time I flew the Raptor. There are no two-seat training versions of the F-22. Although no one else was physically present with me during that glorious first flight in the high-tech stealth jet,

I didn't feel alone. Many fighter pilots had gone before me, feeling the thrill of commanding a highly maneuverable combat aircraft. After experiencing it for myself, I had a better understanding of my predecessors.

Once I was safely on the ground, my thoughts returned to the fighter pilots of yesterday. I wondered if I would experience the same things they did during their flying careers. Would I be able to follow in their footsteps? Would I measure up to the high standard they set?

It's said that those who don't study history are doomed to repeat it. We can learn a lot by reviewing the lives of our ancestors and looking at how they fit into world history. The past never interested me much during my time in high school and college. There always seemed to be something more important going on in the present that kept me from taking the time to look back. All of that changed when I joined the United States Air Force in 2004.

During my time as an active duty fighter pilot, I experienced the past first-hand through fighter pilot traditions that had been handed down over decades. I saw how the combat aviators of old thought and acted and how their conduct and beliefs permeate life in today's fighter squadrons. My desire to study history surged, and I started learning about the aerial warriors of an era gone by.

The more I learned about those crusty old pilots and compared my story to theirs, the deeper the connection I felt to them. Everything in my career seemed to link back in time to those first, brave airborne soldiers who took to the skies in the cutting-edge technology of their day. As my respect for the past intensified, I felt a desire to share my findings with pilots new to the fighter world. I wanted them to feel the pride I felt. I wanted them to appreciate the sacrifices of our flying ancestors the way I did.

No book written can do justice to the greatness of the pioneers of combat aviation. No piece of literature will be able to give the reader an accurate understanding of the uniqueness of life in a fighter squadron. Such vision is gained only by living the traditions and participating in the rituals. Despite the impossible task of passing on a love for our heritage, I have attempted to capture in writing the spirit of the men and women who have protected our skies for nearly a century.

## Why a Book on Tradition?

Fighter pilots are secretive and superstitious creatures. We don't like outsiders digging into our business. However, I wrote this book with the hope of keeping the warrior spirit alive. It is meant to inspire future fighter pilots to find meaning in the past and to conduct themselves in a way that honors our heritage. The next generation must maintain the standard required of one who bears the title *Fighter Pilot*.

Most fighter pilots are taught *the way* during the formative years of their training. You'll see that most of the personal stories related here took place while I was in the early stages of my fighter pilot indoctrination: Undergraduate Pilot Training (UPT), Introduction to Fighter Fundamentals (IFF), the B-Course, and Mission Qualification Training (MQT).

"Why *Piano Burning* as the title?" That's the most frequent question asked of me as I've shared my two-year long project with friends and family. Burning pianos is an age-old fighter pilot tradition, but certainly not the most important of our rituals. Many fighter pilots go their entire careers without ever participating in a burning. As one of many important traditions, piano burnings are a fragment of a puzzle that, when put together with other pieces, creates a beautiful image of past pride, honor, and nobleness. I want to entice readers to examine this "puzzle piece" in hopes that they will desire to turn over the other pieces and put the image together for themselves.

## The Devil's in the Details (So to Speak)

Fighter pilot phraseology can be quite confusing. Like folks in many other career fields, we practically speak our own language. For this reason, I have included a chapter called Fighter Pilot Speak to help clarify some of the terminologies I use in the book. If you run across a term you don't understand, reference the Fighter Pilot Speak chapter, and you'll likely find a definition for the word or phrase in question.

Additionally, this collection of fighter pilot traditions is intended for a broad audience. It's meant for everyone from the little boy or girl who looks up to the sky dreaming of flying a pointy-nose jet to the old, veteran fighter jock wanting to reminisce about the bright days spent walking the halls of a fighter squadron.

Many fighter pilot traditions reflect the rough men who created them, and could easily be given an "R-rating" or worse. The approach taken here is such that the younger audience won't be scared away and the older audience will feel comfortable sharing with their family. Although I have removed most of the harsher language connected with fighter pilot traditions, the lack of profanity in no way changes the traditions themselves or diminishes their greatness. It doesn't matter how the traditions are passed along; the point is to keep them alive.

My focus in this book is on fighter pilot traditions that primarily take place outside of regular working hours. Squadron social life must balance out the stress, hard work, and hours of intense focus and concentration we experience during our long workdays. It may appear from relating some of these social traditions that we are all just a bunch of party animals. Nothing could be further from the truth. You would be hard-pressed to find a more professional group of people operating at such a high level than the fighter pilot community. I'm proud to have been associated with such fine people and will forever treasure my time in the fighter squadron

# Tradition 101

One balmy afternoon in 1944, Captain Robert W. Aschenbrener's world stood still over the South Pacific. Professional athletes often say that time seems to slow when they're in *the zone* the way it did when Neo dodged bullets in the movie *The Matrix*. On this day, Robert Aschenbrener — known to members of the 8th Fighter Squadron as Asch — was in *the zone*.

The distorted perception of time made the Japanese Ki-61Tony in Asch's gun sights an easy target. The propellers of the single-engine, Kawasaki-built aircraft turned in slow motion and slowly disintegrated before his eyes as multiple .50 caliber bullets impacted the enemy fighter. The rounds continued to pick apart the doomed aircraft, tearing through the engine cowling, the canopy and a portion of the left wing. The acrid smell of gunpowder filling Asch's cockpit brought with it memories of his two air-to-air kills nearly a year earlier.

The powerful 12-cylinder Allison engines of Captain Aschenbrener's P-38 Lightning hesitated slightly upon ingesting smoke from the destroyed enemy fighter but continued to march resolutely to the orders of their pilot in command. Asch effortlessly dodged the debris from his slain opponent and turned his sights to a glint of sun reflecting from the canopy of another aircraft: the wingman of his recently fallen enemy.

Over the next several minutes, the sky became a swirling mess of airplanes, smoke, and falling debris punctuated by the occasional parachute. When the day was over, Asch had single-handedly downed four enemy aircraft. Combined with the two previous kills under his belt, Captain Aschenbrener's work on November 24, 1944, would earn him a title won by few aviators: that of *Ace*.

Asch didn't have much time to revel in the glory of his victories, for the work of a fighter pilot is never done. One month after Captain Aschenbrener wreaked havoc on the Japanese Air Force, he found himself over the Philippines executing another demanding mission. Sweat dripped from Asch's brow as he rolled in hot for a Christmas Day strafing run on an anti-aircraft battery at Clark Field.

The airfield, built by the Americans, had been overrun by Japanese forces several months earlier and was now a high priority target in the struggle to turn the tide of the war in the South Pacific. The members of the 8th Fighter Squadron "Black Sheep" had been fighting hard for several months to force the Imperial Army to leave the key island.

Asch had visited the base once before it was taken over by the Japanese. He hardly recognized it now from the air due to the cratered runways and the rubble piles from the hangars damaged in previous attacks.

The sky around the young captain's aircraft was dotted with percussive clouds of black smoke; visible indications of the incendiary rounds fired from the anti-aircraft batteries below. Asch concentrated on locating the source of the incoming fire. The battle-hardened warrior had already made one successful strafing pass on the airfield. Without the element of surprise, his next attack would be much more difficult.

Squinting through the glare of the sun on his canopy, he could barely discern the minuscule gun emplacements from the surrounding rubble of the battered airfield. Asch briefly caught sight of what appeared to be men reloading one of the powerful surface-to-air cannons as he peered through the smoky haze hanging over the field. That split-second view of the target area was all the intrepid fighter pilot needed to plan his strafing run and begin his attack.

Asch sharply banked his P-38 and pulled the nose of the sleek killing machine in the direction of his target. He had about 45 degrees of turn remaining before the gun emplacement would be in his sights. Asch intentionally over-banked the aircraft and set the dive angle for his strafing run. Upon reaching a 30-degree nose-low pitch attitude, and just as he began to roll his aircraft upright, the mighty warplane shuddered as flak from a nearby anti-aircraft round sprayed the P-38's empennage and right side.

Asch had been hit. He wrestled the aircraft out of the dive and turned away from the airfield. The controls were becoming less responsive as the right engine burst into flames. It wouldn't be long before the aircraft was a giant fireball. Captain Aschenbrener trimmed the aircraft for level flight as best he could and slid the canopy back in preparation for bailing out. If he jumped out at his present position, he would immediately be surrounded by the enemy. With the patience of a combat-seasoned aviator, Asch waited until the absolute last moment before he released his restraints and leaped into the air.

Once his body was separated from the crippled aircraft and falling freely towards a rice paddy below, Asch pulled his parachute's ripcord. The opening shock of the canopy vibrated through his body as he watched his once beautiful P-38 impact the ground to become a pile of twisted metal and burning fuel.

For a moment, Asch heard nothing but the rush of the wind around him and the din of the battle raging behind him. For just a moment, there was beauty in the chaos. Asch's mind drifted briefly from the need to prepare for a parachute landing and enjoyed the view of the Philippine landscape below him. Those few seconds of tranquility ended abruptly as he splashed down in an expansive rice paddy. In a tangle of mud and nylon, he tumbled to a stop. His heart racing, Asch scrambled to free himself from the entanglement. At first, his moves to break loose from the twisted lines of his parachute were slow and deliberate. The sound of men cutting through the undergrowth of the nearby forest spurred Asch to work faster. What would happen if he were caught? Would they torture him? Would they kill him? He didn't want to find out and tried to put the thought of failure from his mind.

Just a few more twists and turns and Asch was free. With a small survival kit hanging from his waist, he stumbled through the rice paddy and into the forest opposite the noise of his pursuers. He needed to get some distance between himself and the enemy. Once he had time on his side, he could take a quick rest, get his bearing, and come up with a plan. Fighter pilots have a knack for confronting impossible situations, and Asch was confident he'd find a way out of this mess.

Asch only made it about 100 yards before he stopped. There were noises all around him, but he couldn't tell if they were natural or man-made. He didn't have to wonder for long, as several dark figures emerged from the shadows of the trees; each accompanied by a rifle pointed at directly at Asch.

One man walked up to the captain, looked him over, and shouted something to the others in a language foreign to Asch. Slowly, the armed men lowered their firearms, and a young boy approached the downed fighter pilot.

"You are American?" asked the boy. Asch didn't speak, his eyes darting nervously around the group of his captors.

"It's ok. We are no Japanese. We are the Huks! Come with us; we can help you."

The Huk Guerillas were a group of communist resistance fighters. They didn't like Americans much, but they liked the Japanese even less. The Huk had decided that helping the Americans was the lesser of two evils. The group roamed the jungles fighting the Japanese and helping downed pilots like Asch whenever they could.

Robert Aschenbrener would spend the next 27 days with the Huk Guerillas evading the Imperial Army before being safely returned to a U.S. naval vessel. Over the course of his time with the Huk, Asch would be joined by several other American aviators who were also on the run. Among the other downed pilots was Alexander Vraciu, a U.S. Navy F-6F Hellcat ace, who became fast friends with Captain Aschenbrener.

Following his triumphant return to the Black Sheep, Asch could have easily gone back to the States to rest from the traumatic experience of being shot out of the sky and being on the run for nearly a month. Instead, Asch did what every self-respecting fighter pilot would do: he asked to get back in the cockpit.

After his request to remain in combat, *Captain* Aschenbrener became *Major* Aschenbrener and assumed command of the Black Sheep's sister squadron: the 7th

Fighter Squadron "Screamin' Demons." He would serve nearly another year of combat before retiring with 345 combat missions under his belt and 850 combat flying hours.

You would think that just being an ace fighter pilot and a combat-hardened veteran was enough to call Robert Aschenbrener a true American hero. But Asch had one last act of fighter pilot awesomeness to perform; one that was unrelated to combat, but demonstrated how this alpha dog approached life.

On August 20, 1945—about eight months after he returned from his time evading with the Huk Guerillas—Robert Aschenbrener went back to Clark Field, which had been reclaimed by American forces. He was accompanied by Ms. Laura Ann Middleton, whom he married on a spot just a couple of miles from where his crippled P-38 had impacted the ground less than a year earlier. Talk about establishing dominance!

For me, flying fighters isn't just a career, it's a way of life. Any of my cohorts will tell you that. Being a part of this exclusive fraternity changes your outlook on life and leaves a deep mark upon your soul.

The fighter lifestyle is one steeped in tradition. New members of this unique circle must learn its history and carry on its traditions, for they will be the ones to instill pride in the future generations of pilots that follow them.

## A Modern-Day Rarity

There are precious few fighter pilots in the world today. Not everyone is cut out to fly fast, high-tech fighter jets. Few people are physically and mentally capable of executing tactics and making life or death decisions under pressure. Additionally, many pilots capable of flying fighters choose not to do so in favor of a different, more relaxed lifestyle. Being a fighter pilot is a combination of choice, capability, and aircraft availability.

I saw a remarkable increase in non-flying-related tasks over the last two years I spent on active duty. Support functions were being consolidated and, in some cases, eliminated altogether. My comrades and I were picking up more ground responsibilities leaving less time to concentrate on maintaining flying proficiency. It was during those twilight years of my full-time military career that I truly understood our plight.

Additionally, tighter defense budgets and improved technology have united to become an insurmountable force in decreasing the number of existing fighter cockpits. The more capable a fighter jet becomes, the more expensive it is, and fewer of them are purchased. Today's fighter acquisition scenario is a weird spin on combat *economies of scale*. Regardless of how powerful the radar is or how effective the stealth technology, a fighter jet is only as capable as the individual piloting it. So, what will become of the fighter pilot? Will the fighter cockpit of the future be unmanned? Is our breed of combat aviator a thing of the past?

Although the future of high-speed jet-jockeys may be in question, one thing is sure: we must retain the same attributes our predecessors exemplified and that have proven successful through decades of combat air campaigns. So how are these vital attributes learned? How is the fighter pilot mentality preserved? There is one simple answer that you won't find on any Pentagon reports or in tactics manuals. The aggressive fighter pilot attitude is preserved and passed on through the observance of *tradition*.

The process of indoctrinating a fledgling fighter pilot is a lengthy one that can span the pilot's career. It starts by teaching the young pilots history and helping them gain the tactical knowledge they will need in combat. The process continues as they prove themselves worthy through study and work and are permitted to participate in rituals like Roll Call and piano burnings. Their acceptance into the fold is culminated by a naming ceremony where they receive a tactical call sign by which they'll be known throughout their career.

The process of being allowed entrance into our exclusive club is required to get everyone on the same page mentally and emotionally. Collectively, we are always looking towards the future while retaining a bright recollection of the past. We honor those who have gone before us by emulating their noble characters and adopting their attributes. We set a high standard of excellence. It is to this end we study the greatness of past combat aviators and examine our ties to previous generations of fighter pilots.

## A Peculiar Breed

Fighter pilots do things that may seem a little strange to the average observer. We point with our elbows, we say things like *cranium* instead of *head*, and we carry large, Round Metal Objects (RMO—our term for a coin) everywhere we go. These things may seem like mere quirks, but to the fighter pilot, they are so much more. Camaraderie formed in the fighter squadron follows us into combat. These little "quirks" help form bonds that instill trust and loyalty — essential elements for any squadron during a time of war.

---

*One day a wise father approached his young son and asked, "Son, what are your thoughts on the future?"*

*The son's face lit up as he turned to his father and smiled, "I want to be a fighter pilot when I grow up!"*

*The sage elder shook his head sadly and replied, "I'm sorry boy, you can't do both."*

---

The American Fighter Pilot is a rare sort: part rebel, part intellectual, part athlete — all kid. If you don't ever want to grow up, become a fighter pilot. However, being an aerial assassin in today's military is not all fun and games. We work harder than we've ever worked.

Tactics continually evolve as technology changes. We're spending more time than ever in the books digesting new and ever-changing information. Budgetary constraints are driving manning shortfalls across the military, which means we don't have the support that was available in the past. In addition to normal flying duties, we find ourselves behind the desk more frequently. Workdays consisting of 12 hours or more are the baseline.

Despite the distractions from flying, not to mention the constant balancing of work and family life, one thing remains constant: our deep devotion to tradition.

This dedication to the past makes sense; we are, after all, creatures of habit. We cling to doing certain things in a certain way, and thus our personalities naturally gravitate toward honoring traditions. But habit isn't the only reason we act the way we do. Our profession is a noble one, established by master aviators who took great strides to set a strong precedent.

### Origins of Tradition

World War I saw the first wide employment of air power in support of military objectives. It stands to reason that the fighter pilot cut his teeth in the skies over Europe. Many fighter pilot traditions were born in the ranks of the British Royal Air Force (RAF) and subsequently passed on to the American pilots who came to join them in their efforts. British influence is seen in the traditions we honor to this day. Regardless of whether you are a British or American pilot flying for the Air Force or the Navy, you are part of a noble heritage of courageous flyers.

It is important to note that the United States Air Force and Navy each may view similar traditions in a different light. While this book focuses on the fighter pilot traditions honored by the United States Air Force, it is worth considering that each American flying service — Air Force and Navy — have had a significant influence on the traditions of the other. In today's joint environment we work closely with each other and are required to place our trust in one another on a regular basis. Friendly competition and increased interaction are starting to blur the lines previously delineating the two services.

The chain connecting today's fighter pilots to those of the past is certainly not perfect. Many traditions die out or change over time if they are not passed on correctly. Some of our rituals have even been specifically prohibited by those in leadership positions.

Due to its mostly word-of-mouth nature, the history of fighter pilot traditions is delicate and somewhat hazy. I asked several Air Force Historians to help identify the genesis of various fighter pilot rituals and lore. With only a handful of written fighter pilot memoirs addressing our sacred heritage (some of which contradict each other), the historians were unable to provide solid answers. It is entirely up to the current group of fighter pilots to ensure subsequent generations are properly indoctrinated into the traditions to keep them from fading away completely.

*"Fighter pilot is an attitude. It is cockiness. It is aggressiveness. It is self-confidence. It is a streak of rebelliousness, and it is competitiveness. But there's something else — there's a spark. There's a desire to be good. To do well; in the eyes of your peers, and in your own mind."*

**- Robin Olds** (From *Fighter Pilot: The Memoirs of Legendary Ace Robin Olds*)

—

## Traditions Under Attack

Over the past several years, many fighter pilot traditions have come under attack. The fighter pilots of yesterday didn't work under the constraints of political correctness. They told it like it was and made fun of *everyone*. They had thick skins and expected everyone else to have the same.

Today's professional environment is different. People get upset when their delicate sensitivities are offended. Fighter pilots have had to tone down their bluntness and take on a gentler, milder persona to avoid being the subject of investigations and lawsuits. The result of this drive toward political correctness is that some traditions are slowly being abandoned. Fear of legal retribution is driving the disposal of a great deal of history!

In 2012, a herculean effort was undertaken by Air Force leadership to clean up flying squadrons (not just fighter squadrons) around the Air Force. Historic patches were stripped from the walls of the proud squadrons they represented if they even hinted at anything inappropriate or offensive. Roll Calls were prohibited in certain squadrons. Hard drives were indiscriminately searched and wiped clean of non-work-related files. It was a cleanse needed to bring the Air Force up to the times, but it may have gone a little too far. It would seem the baby has, unfortunately, been thrown out with the proverbial bathwater.

Some things, however, haven't changed and never will. The spirit of the fighter pilot is as bright as it ever was. The men and women of today's fighter squadrons push themselves harder than ever to achieve greatness. Pride, courage, and aggressiveness have never been stronger. In a high operational tempo like we have today, these attributes *must* be present. Without them, today's fighter pilot won't last.

# Friday in the Fast Jet Business

It was a busy week full of long days flying fast jets. I was a brand-new flight lead and had spent the bulk of my time mission planning, studying, and practicing my briefs. I had several items piling up on my to-do list in the Training Shop, but those would have to wait. Today was Friday. In true Friday fashion, the squadron was going to shake things up by kicking off a *Combat Friday*.

The only schedule published Thursday afternoon was our Friday morning show time. We weren't told who would be flying or what mission we would execute. The intent of a Combat Friday is to plan as you would in a real-world combat scenario: at the least minute with minimal preparation.

Gringo, our squadron's weapons officer, was beaming ear-to-ear as my squadron mates and I filed into the briefing room and closed the door.

"All right," said Gringo. His booming voice commanded attention, helping us shake off any remnants of sleep in the early hour.

"Here's how we're going to roll. Shotz, you're our Blue Air flight lead today," continued Gringo. I felt a rush of excitement at having been chosen to lead the gaggle!

"Your wingmen will be Lite, Quake, and Rum. On the Red side: Edge, Jolt, Bandit, and Gordo. Your Blue Air mission is Surface Attack; here is your Air Tasking Order complete with your assigned targets."

The Weapons Officer, also known as *the Patch* for the unmistakable Weapons School Graduate patch on his left shoulder, doled out several pages of information to each pilot participating in the fight. We all gazed at the papers with the same stare a deer gives into oncoming headlights.

"You step in one hour," said Gringo. "Use your time wisely."

I gathered the other members of my flight to begin mission planning. We quickly pulled the target coordinates from our tasking and one of my wingmen began plotting them on a map. Our targets were all located in the middle of a surface-to-air missile (SAM) engagement zone. Apparently, the airborne threat wouldn't be the only thing harassing us today.

My number three wingman, Lite, was my Deputy Mission Commander and would be assisting me in devising the tactical game plan we would use to reach the target area. With limited time to plan, I had to rely heavily on tactics and contracts in our F-22 *Tactics, Techniques, and Procedures* manual. Most of the tactical decision making and game plan modification would take place real-time in the airspace.

Minutes after we completed our preflight huddle, we stepped out to the jets. Shortly after, my four-ship rumbled down the runway, getting airborne for what would shape up to be an epic Friday morning mission. It wasn't long before systems checks were completed and the fight was on.

"Warlord, picture," I said on the radio. My request was answered by our Command and Control (C2) for the day, call sign *Warlord*.

"Raptor 1, Warlord, picture: four groups capping," came the reply.

C2 continued to give location information and a declaration of *Hostile* to each of the groups holding near our target area. The four hostile Raptors, simulating enemy fighters on Red Air, were all flown by experienced Instructor Pilots who couldn't wait to keep us from reaching our objective.

I glanced at the aircraft clock. It was almost push time. I cleared my four-ship to Raptor Tactical, a beyond visual range formation that would put us all a little over 10 nautical miles apart and line abreast.

"Raptor 1, push," I called over the radio. We were on our way into bad-guy land.

As the enemy fighters committed out of their CAPs (Combat Air Patrols — tactically placed holding locations) my Blue Air fighters went to work targeting the air threat. Within minutes, each member of my flight had missiles in the air. In training, the missiles are simulated and an onboard computer calculates the fly-out time an actual missile would have based on the launch conditions.

"Raptor 1, kill bullseye 3-2-0, 8, 20,000," I said as I keyed the radio mic switch. My radio call conveyed the bearing, range, and altitude of the enemy fighter that just soaked up my missile shot.

"Mig 1, copy kill," came the reply.

Each Blue Air fighter called his kill, and soon the airspace was clear of the threat. Now we just had to worry about the SAMs awaiting us near the target.

I cleared my four-ship to the pre-briefed attack formation in preparation for our target run. Within minutes, we each dropped our bombs, turned around, and began executing a maneuver called a SAM Weave to defeat any missiles coming up at us from the ground.

As we turned back towards our egress point, my aircraft began to locate and identify enemy jets along our route of flight. Low on weapons and fuel, the egress was going to be interesting — the enemy wasn't going to let us off easily.

We spent the next several minutes fighting like mad to clear up the air picture. Now I saw why our bandits were easy kills as we worked our way to the target. They wanted to be set up for the real challenge of the egress.

As we pointed home, we were forced to merge with several of the fighters and found ourselves in multiple ACM engagements (Air Combat Maneuvers — a visual fight involving multiple aircraft). In the end, we all fought bravely and made it out alive. The mission wasn't perfect, and mistakes were made. But we bombed the target, and we all came home.

Back in the briefing room, each Blue Air player was all grins as we played back the mission on a large, overhead screen. Our debrief wasn't the standard hours-long ordeal that was the norm during the rest of the week. It was Friday, and we still had a lot to do.

No matter how difficult the week, all the thrashing and flailing is worth it come Friday. Friday in the fast jet business is magical. It gives us a brief respite from the week's relentless pace.

You may find it hard to believe that being a fighter pilot is work. You may wonder why Fridays are so special if we just spend the rest of the week performing loops to music and partying in the squadron bar. Don't let Hollywood fool you. A day in the life of a fighter pilot is not all fun-and-games as Maverick and Goose from the movie *Top Gun* would have you believe. If it were, here's how your day would look:

## Typical Day for Maverick and Goose

- *0800* (or 0830, who's keeping track?) - Don your sunglasses and leather jacket, and ride your motorcycle to work (be sure to fist-pump any aircraft that may be shooting a practice approach or taking off.)
- *0900ish* - Meet up with a room full of bros for a pre-flight briefing filled with antics, flirty smack talk, and words from the commander telling you that whatever mission you are about to do is the most important mission you'll ever fly.
- *1000* - Walk to your aircraft in slow motion. No one needs earplugs because hearing damage doesn't happen when walking by running jet engines with your sunglasses on. It just doesn't.
- *1030* - Put on your "serious face" as you perform loops to music. The whifferdill, combined with speed brakes, is the secret to dogfighting. There's no known defense; it works every time.
- *1100* - High-five your back-seater as you head to the locker room for a leisurely hot shower full of more smack talk and lounging around.
- *1200* - Pop some gum in your mouth and head to the debrief where your blatant violation of training rules and disregard for safety of flight is praised as the "Gutsiest move I ever saw."
- *1230* - Grab some baby oil and Levi's (not blue jeans — legitimate Levi's) and hit the sand for some shirtless beach volleyball.

- *1245* - Ditch the game to spend the rest of the day chasing girls and drinking (not necessarily in that order.)

## The Reality

Life in the fighter community is much less glamorous than Maverick and Goose would have you believe. If you're not working a twelve-hour day, you're probably on a non-flying assignment working a desk job. So, here's what a day's agenda looks like for a real fighter pilot:

- *0445* - Walk through the door to the squadron exactly twelve hours after you last left. On days that you fly, you must meet the minimum twelve-hour pilot rest requirement. You check weather and NOTAMs (Notices to Airmen), and you are in place for the training mission brief five minutes before it starts.
- *0500* - Blink the sleep out of your eyes as the Mission Commander begins the mass coordination brief. Pilots of every aircraft participating in the fight are required to be present so that everyone understands the mission and expectations. If you are one second late, you either open the door and enter the brief in shame, or you wait outside. Being late to anything is an egregious sin.
- *0700* - Work through various maintenance-related aircraft issues to ensure you get airborne in a fully mission-capable jet. Once you have taken to the

skies, your focus is so intent on the mission that you fail to notice the beauty of the world below. There's no time for sightseeing.

- *0810* - You join up with your tanker for air-to-air refueling before the mission starts. The tanker crew has located the only weather in the airspace and refuses to fly in the clear air immediately adjacent to the clouds. You struggle to stay visual with the tanker as your wingman repeatedly falls out of position with the tanker's refueling boom, prolonging your pain.

- *0830* - You are barely able to make the start of the fight on time. Your Situation Display shows a blob of hostile aircraft headed your way. Great. The adversaries are sending a gorilla package your way (numerous aircraft bunched up in one piece of sky) with lots of radar jamming. Have fun sorting through that chocolate mess. You'll probably take a Fox 1 to the face (slang for getting shot by an enemy missile) in the process of targeting that delightful little gift.

- *0910* - Grit your teeth and say a few choice words under your breath when your wingman bingos out (runs out of gas) and goes home. Uh oh, you should have checked your gas — you're at bingo fuel as well.

- *0930* - Get your wheels on the ground and debrief with maintenance immediately after you land. Ensure the maintainers have all the information they need to fix the minor (or major) issues you experienced with the aircraft while airborne. Endure their harassment as they blame you for everything that's wrong with the jet.

- *1015* - Begin reviewing your mission by watching your *tapes*. Tape review consists of watching information presented to you by the cockpit displays while airborne. Make note of any missile or gun shots that were taken and see if there was any data you didn't glean while airborne. Oops, those few choice words you thought you said under your breath were caught on the intercom recording. I guess you won't be looking your wingman in the eye during this debrief.

- *1130* - Attend the air-to-air shot evaluation where you will confirm the locations and types of aircraft against which you employed training ordnance. It seems that one of the kills you claimed airborne wasn't valid after all. You rummage through your wallet to see if you have cash to pay the requisite $5 for erroneous kill calls. Are you having fun yet?

- *1200* - Your initial wave of morning caffeine has worn off, and your eyelids are beginning to droop as the adversaries clear off and you start your flight debrief. On average, you will spend two to four hours further reviewing tapes (in front of your flight mates) and discussing tactical employment to eliminate future mistakes. You pretend you don't see your wingman as he glares at you after hearing what you said about him on your tapes.

- *1600* - You're not flying tomorrow, so the twelve-hour pilot rest rule doesn't apply. You must now finish writing that Officer Performance Report that was due a week ago, but you haven't had time to write with the new tactics manual you're expected to memorize. You debate whether you should finish it or study the new employment parameters for one of your weapons. I guess the performance report can wait a few more days.

- *1800* - You consider going home for the day, but you've already missed dinner so you might as well read that new Flight Crew Information File that just came out about the changes to the airfield taxi diagram. Oh, crap, you forgot to call the Finance Office to discuss a problem with your pay. They closed shop at 1600, so no one will be there now. You better make a note to do that tomorrow.

- *1900* - Time to go for a quick run. You need to shave a few seconds off your mile-and-a-half run time so you pass your fitness test with a 90 percent or greater next week. If you can't make it happen, you'll be running it again in six months.

- *2000* - You finally walk through the door of your house. Your four-year-old son runs up and punches you in the crotch as your exhausted wife stuffs your one-year-old daughter (who has a dirty diaper) into your arms so she can get the dinner she's been keeping warm for you off the stove. You decide to give your wife a break since she has been fighting her dogfight all day, long after running out of fuel and weapons.

- 2200 - You better get to bed. Mission planning starts tomorrow at 0600 for a complicated new mission designed by the Weapons Officer in which you will be leading a total of twenty aircraft. Congrats dude, you're living the dream.

If there were a day of the week in the life of a *real* fighter pilot that comes remotely close to a day in the lives of Maverick and Goose, it would be Friday. Friday in the fast jet business is a great day to be alive. The fighter squadron seems to lighten up a little. The intense focus, rushed schedules, and long hours seem to fade into the background on Friday.

On Friday, we don our squadron morale shirts designed by the LPA (Lieutenant Protection Association) in the squadron colors. We replace our shoulder patches with a squadron heritage patch (a design from the past) on the right shoulder. A patch denoting your status as a qualified fighter pilot replaces the Wing patch on your left shoulder (unless you're a graduate of Weapons School.) We switch out our nametags for one that has only our tactical call sign.

We usually only fly once on Friday morning. The missions are a little more fun as we take off some of the training handcuffs with which we normally fight. Most Fridays don't leave time for a lengthy debrief. Post-mission duties are usually kept to only an hour so as not to interfere with the Burger Burn at lunchtime.

The Burger Burn is the opportunity for the LPA to proudly display their culinary abilities — the only skill set they possess that can be appreciated by other fighter pilots in the squadron. Trust me; no one is impressed with their flying.

After the Burger Burn, everyone gathers back in the vault for a Weapons and Tactics Talk, affectionately known as a WATT. The WATT usually lasts only an hour or two and resembles the academic setting of a college campus. The big differences being that everyone is wearing a flight suit, everyone has a drink in hand, and everyone is stuffing their face with jalapeño popcorn — a staple of the fighter squadron. Intel will often start the WATT with a quick Current Intel Brief before turning it over to the Patch.

The Weapons Officer goes to great lengths to ensure each pilot is fully up to speed on current tactics and that we are all on the same page with pilots from other squadrons. This hour or two is well spent and is considered sacred; no one wants to be *that guy* who doesn't know what's going on.

Once everyone has been tactically enlightened at the WATT, the meeting is turned over to the Director of Operations (DO) for the pilot meeting. Pilot meetings — affectionately called *pirate meetings* in an attempt at Friday humor — are different from WATTs as they cover non-tactical items pertaining to the operations of the squadron.

With the WATT and pilot meeting out of the way, it is time to turn up the socializing at Roll Call. The pent-up rage, frustration, and stress of the week come out during Roll Call as squadron members tell stories, sing songs, and imbibe a broad range of beverages. Fridays are like clockwork. You can set your watch by the Friday schedule in a fighter squadron.

We work hard as fighter pilots. Constant military exercises and long deployments take their toll on you if you don't find a way to relax and let your hair down occasionally. Friday social activities are a small, but vital part of life in a fighter squadron. If you don't happen to find yourself in a fighter squadron on Friday, don't worry. "Friday in the Fast Jet Business" is more a state of mind than anything else. It's a time to enjoy friends, talk about flying, and tell everyone else how great you are. Last I checked, you don't have to be in a fighter squadron to do that, but it sure helps.

# Roll Call

"HACK!!!" our esteemed Mayor cried out, as the door to the squadron bar slammed shut. The bar, known during the day as the *Squadron Heritage Room,* fell silent. It was the end of another work-week in the squadron, and it was time to revel in one of the oldest fighter pilot traditions: Roll Call.

Mac, one of the flight leads in my squadron, stood at the head of the bar eyeing a list of the squadron's pilots while taking a deep draw from his squadron mug. The over-sized yellow sport coat he wore over his military uniform — the customary garb of the Black Sheep Mayor — contrasted sharply with the sea of green flight suits in the room. No one in the squadron was on leave or out sick; the house was packed.

He looked to Ripple, who stood to his left holding the *Doofer Book.* Ripple, Mac's Scribe, gave him a nod and raised his pencil to a blank, open page. Without another word, Mac began reading the names on his list. Roll Call had officially begun.

Trust and camaraderie are essential components in any combat unit. A good leader knows how important it is for the warriors in his or her unit to be willing to go to war together and to die for each other if necessary. Roll Call is a tradition meant to strengthen the bonds of brotherhood in a fighter squadron. (**Yes, this includes our female fighter pilot sisters!**) It is intended to create an atmosphere that breeds trust and friendship amongst the pilots. Such traditions are essential to the morale and wellbeing of a combat fighter squadron.

## Origin and Evolution of Roll Call

The tradition of Roll Call is one of the oldest in the Air Force and springs from the early days of combat aviation. Before fighter pilots flew with radios, they relied on keeping sight of their flight mates and maximized the use of visual signals. If you lost visual contact with the other members of your flight, you would attempt to rejoin based on a little planning and a lot of luck. You would likely be alone for the duration of the mission if you lost sight of the other members of your flight! Worse, if a flight member were shot down, no one would know until the downed pilot was overdue for return from the mission. So, to ascertain combat losses, commanders would call their pilots together at the end of a day of combat and take roll. Those not attending Roll Call were then considered missing or killed in action.

I imagine Roll Call was not an easy time for the pilots in attendance. They had to accept the losses of their brethren, then turn around and fly back into combat the next day. They managed to deal with the deaths of their friends and brothers the best they could. As methods for determining combat losses improved, Roll Call was no longer needed for accountability. Instead, it became a way to increase camaraderie.

Since those early days of combat aviation, fighter squadrons have been putting their own twists on Roll Call. Some of the tweaks and changes have taken root while others have fallen by the wayside. Today's fighter pilot Roll Call is a conglomeration of decades of fighter pilot traditions and shenanigans. The one thing that has not changed is the intent of fostering brotherhood.

## The Mayor

Today's fighter pilot Roll Call follows a loose outline. It is led by the Mayor — the lynchpin of squadron morale. The coveted role of the Mayor is to guide the rowdy mass of fighter pilots through an agenda of calling roll, telling jokes and stories, and singing songs. He can be appointed in various ways, but a younger fighter pilot (most likely a young captain) usually fills the role. It is typically someone who has established him or herself in the squadron both tactically and socially. In most squadrons, an election is held after one or more people have been nominated for the position.

At various intervals during the Roll Call, the Mayor's authority must be challenged by the bros

37

chanting, "THE MAYOR HAS LOST CONTROL! THE MAYOR HAS LOST CONTROL!" The Mayor must then reestablish dominance by whatever means necessary — usually by yelling and throwing things — and quell the uprising by making the mutinous group imbibe the *Nectar of the Gods*, (Another name for *Jeremiah Weed* whiskey) or a suitable replacement.

The Mayor must be able to outlast and outwit every other person in the bar. Not all Mayors can fulfill the demanding role. Mac was the epitome of a Mayor: bold, witty, and full of energy. He could dance like a monkey when he thought the crowd was fading and pull us right back into the fun. One of his best mayoral attributes was his ability to think on the fly.

We were a solid hour into one particularly fateful Roll Call when Mac paused to look at his script. When he began speaking again, words weren't the only thing that spewed forth from his mouth. Yup, you guessed it; he had max-performed his stomach and a toxic mixture of booze, pizza, and who-knows-what-else proceeded to douse both his notes and the bros in his immediate vicinity. The laughing and horseplay came to a screeching halt as all eyes were focused on him to assess his follow-on actions.

"Well, that was embarrassing," said Mac with a smile on his face. He shook the debris from his script and picked up right where he left off as cheers filled the room. He had triumphantly overcome adversity under the judging eyes of the room. Even those on the receiving end of the blowout were impressed and seemed not to care. A good Mayor can make or break Roll Call. Only the strong survive.

## Alcohol and the Fighter Pilot

Before we go any further, I need to say a quick word about alcohol consumption in the fighter squadron. Fighter pilots — while rebellious, defiant, and aggressive — know their limits and look out for each other. Each is expected to moderate his intake of alcohol or have it moderated for him. If the occasion calls for one guy to have an *awesome time,* then someone usually sees to it that he makes him home safely. Whether or not his significant other kills him is his problem.

Alcohol consumption is not *required* in the fighter pilot bar. Many fighter pilots today choose not to drink for a variety of reasons. For the non-drinkers, "unleaded" shots are poured at Roll Call. The non-alcoholic shots usually consist of a nasty concoction involving jalapeño juice (an ingredient that is readily available for the making of popcorn), Diet Coke, and anything else easily accessible. I took a shot once that had salad dressing and chicken grease in the mix. Yum.

## What to Expect

The agenda of Roll Call is relatively uniform throughout the tactical community, but each squadron puts a personal spin on the ritual. Roll Call begins promptly at a time that coincides with the squadron's designation (i.e. the 27th Fighter Squadron would begin Roll Call at 16:27.) When the Mayor yells "HACK," anyone that passes through the door, even if only a fraction of a second late, must pay the toll. The price of such a heinous act as being late is outlined by the rules of the bar, but normally involves a shot of Jeremiah Weed.

For those who have yet to attend a Roll Call, the agenda may look something like this:

- Hack
- Calling of Roll
- Introduction of Guests to the Bar
- Official Business
- Upgrades
- Firsts
- Overspeeds and Over-Gs
- Instant Justice (IJ)
- Tribute to Fallen Warriors
- Stories and Jokes
- Songs
- Adjourn

Once Roll Call has started with the *Hack*, the official roll is called by the Mayor, who may delegate this duty to the Scribe. Anyone not present, and who has not made prior arrangements with the Mayor for their absence, will be assessed a $1 fine on their Snack-O tab. As mentioned earlier, late arrivals must pay a price, usually by toasting the bar with a "tasty" shot.

Guests to the bar must come bearing gifts and are introduced by someone who knows the guest relatively well. The pilot who introduces the guest must also demonstrate the squadron toast. If anyone, including the guest, messes up the squadron toast at any point during the night, they are required to make amends.

Once the guests have imparted their gifts, several more segments of Roll Call follow that require gifts to the bar for various reasons. You must provide a bottle of your favorite beverage for completing an upgrade, doing something for the first time (like shooting a missile or sitting SOF), breaking a jet, or for any other reason deemed necessary by the Mayor.

With the bar fully stocked, the remaining segments of Roll Call typically involve the assessment of fines (in the form of *leaded* or *unleaded* shots.) The offender of an IJ, the teller of a joke (whether it's funny or not), and people on whom a story is told must all pass muster with the Shotmeister before Roll Call can continue.

There is a solemn portion of Roll Call. We always pause to remember our fallen brothers, those who have "paid the ultimate price." We raise a toast to those who have gone before, and those who won't be coming back. This segment of Roll Call pays homage to the Roll Calls of yore and may be the only time a fighter pilot shows any emotion other than *awesomeness*. Before the mood gets too somber, the Mayor will open the bar to stories.

Stories are the crux of the gathering; they can make or break a Roll Call. We make fun of each other for stupid things that were done or said during the week. Only in a facility as secure as the squadron bar are TDY (Temporary Duty or Temporary Duty Yonder) stories told. (We'll discuss why that is later.) The best stories usually come out at the first Roll Call after a TDY!

When the storytelling is finished, each story is summarized by the Scribe and put before the masses for a vote as to which was the best. Typically, the person about whom the winning story was told will get an award — something along the lines of a *Donkey Award*. The name of the award differs from one unit to the next. In the 8th Fighter Squadron, we called it the *Goat Award*; if you did something unbecoming of a Black Sheep, you were a goat. The only rule when telling a story in the bar is that it must contain at least 10% truth. Other than that, anything goes provided it's entertaining.

Once the applause-o-meter (typically acted out by a lieutenant) has indicated a story winner, Roll Call is closed out with the singing of songs. Some fighter pilot songs are about combat flying and are deeply rooted in tradition. Others have origins outside of the service and have nothing to do with flying, and everything to do with booze and women. Some squadrons have a hymnbook from which the freshmen class may learn the songs and understand some of the rituals. Songs are such a large part of fighter pilot bar life that I've dedicated a chapter to them later in the book.

Fighter pilot singing is one of the traditions that has recently come under fire by military leadership for being politically incorrect and offensive. In fact, the whole tradition of Roll Call is being threatened as we speak. As the cultural climate of the Air Force changes (after all, this is a "kinder, gentler" Air Force), so do the traditions of fighter pilots. There have been several allegations made against fighter squadron commanders for not maintaining a professional atmosphere by allowing rowdy, offensive Roll Calls to take place. In response, some commanders have canceled Roll Calls altogether.

## Fight Like Boyd

In today's climate, the sky is not the only arena in which we must struggle. Wing conference rooms and the offices of commanders are fraught with peril. These monolithic arenas have always been battlegrounds for the fighter pilot. Struggling for our way of life amid bureaucracy is nothing new to us. Our success rate, sadly, is not quite as good on the ground as it is in the sky.

As a community, we would do well to apply some of the same tactics we use to win dogfights to the battles we fight for our traditions. If we could argue as well as Col John Boyd could dogfight, we'd be in great shape.

Col Boyd was known as "Forty-Second Boyd" for an ongoing bet he had with members of his squadron. The gist of the bet was this: Boyd would welcome any challenger to a dogfight, and if they could gun him down in forty seconds, he would pay them forty dollars. To make the bet more tantalizing to potential takers, he volunteered to start out in a defensive position.

Without fail, Boyd would serve his opponents a fresh helping of bullets (theoretical ones, of course) in the allotted time or less. He did this by having a superior understanding of aircraft performance and how it played into the geometry of the fight. At times, Boyd would aggressively bleed energy to cause his opponent to push out in front of him. (No, Maverick, he didn't pop the speed brakes. Put them away.) At other times, he would sustain his energy and count on the turn circle geometry to work itself out in such a way that he could transition to the offensive. This processes of depleting, sustaining, and gaining energy was something he worked into a model called the *Energy-Maneuverability Theory*.

Like Boyd, we need to manage our *energy*. We must know the appropriate circumstances in which to start a defensive break turn or sustain our energy as we are faced with issues brought about by cultural climate change. As fighter pilots, we must adapt and find new ways to keep timeless traditions like Roll Call alive.

The squadrons of which I have been a part seem to have adjusted wisely to the ever-shifting corporate landscape. Squadrons conduct an "audience appropriate" Roll Call based on who is in attendance. When it's just the bros, it's as rowdy and awesome as always (think *energy-depleting break turn*.) When outsiders are in attendance, it's toned down as a defensive measure (think *energy-sustaining turn*.)

Whether it's a push-it-up Roll Call lasting well into the night, or just a quick, harmless get-together, the purpose remains the same: to boost morale and bring the unit closer together. Without a tight connection amongst squadron members, trust and comradery become strained in a time of war. Fighter pilot traditions like Roll Call are sacred, and help the squadron become a better, more effective combat unit.

# Song and the Fighter Pilot

Fighter pilots pride themselves on their uncanny singing abilities. We are, after all, good at everything. These talents are magically made manifest after a drink or three in the sanctuary of the squadron bar and must be performed at maximum volume with sheer exuberance. At times the songs are led by the unnamed wingmen in the squadron purely for entertainment purposes. Other times, most everyone aggressively joins in. So why does music have such a prominent place in the fighter squadron bar? Where did the songs originate?

## Origins of our Hymns

Most of what I will refer to as the *real* fighter pilot songs (songs that were written by fighter pilots about fighter pilots) seem to have originated after World War II. Deployed fighter pilots in those days didn't have Wi-Fi in their tents, FaceTime dates with their spouses, or a two-drink per day limit. In those days, they had a squadron bar to help them fill any downtime. Many of them got creative and used song as a venue to complain about their situation. Several of those songs took root and thrive in the squadron bar to this day.

The refrains sung in bars across the Air Force are of various origins. Many of the beloved melodies we croon have roots outside of the fighter community. Pretty much any good drinking song has, at some point, been modified slightly to fit fighter pilot lifestyle. Many young wingmen don't realize this, and I was one of them.

It was August 2006, and I was a young 1st Lieutenant living the aviator dream life. I had just arrived at work when one of my buddies rushed into the room beaming.

"Hey dude, get your gear on, we're going to Spokane for the weekend!" he exclaimed.

My buddy, Shadow, informed me that he was taking a jet for a static display at an air show in Spokane, Washington, and the guy who originally wanted to go with him was sick and fell out at the last minute. Of course, I was in! Without time to go home and pack a bag, I grabbed my gear, jumped in the jet, and we were off.

Once on the ground in Spokane, we made a quick stop at the mall where I purchased some clothes for the weekend, and then we headed off to a nice little bar and grill downtown. As the evening wore on, the dinner crowd left, and the drinking crowd arrived. It was just before we settled our bill that we heard the recognizable strains of a tender melody we had sung many times in our squadron bar. Our faces lit up—fellow fighter pilots were present!

We rushed over in the direction of the singing to find a group of about 20 young men merrily singing the chorus to the familiar refrain. We joined right in and were immediately accepted into the group. Upon finishing the song, there was a lot of laughing, back slapping, and hand shaking. Shadow approached the guy who had led the group in song and asked which squadron they were in and where they were from. I'll never forget the look on the guy's face.

"Squadron? You mean like... military? No bro, we're a rugby team!"

My heart sank as it dawned on me that the traditions I had come to embrace originated somewhere other than the fighter community. Shadow and I left that night reeling from the experience and trying to understand what had just happened.

To avoid similar experiences, I decided to do a little research on the situation and found that many of the songs currently being sung in our bar were not ours. In fact, many of the songs were much more recent than the "old tradition" led me to believe. Certainly, many songs have been written by fighter pilots, but let's face it— fighter pilots have other things to do than sit around and write music.

## Evolution of Song

The 8th Fighter Squadron gave me a true indoctrination into the world of fighter pilot tradition. The Black Sheep, as the squadron is known, has a rich history of combat fighter pilots who have downed enemy fighters all around the globe. I was thrilled to learn that a squadron member from the Korean War era would be present at an upcoming squadron reunion we were hosting. It was at that reunion I learned the meaning of history and tradition. It was at the Black Sheep reunion that I truly learned what a fighter pilot song is!

In the early '80s, the Black Sheep were flying the mighty F-15C, an aircraft relatively new to the Air Force at the time. Despite massive time constraints, several members of the Black Sheep got together and formed a squadron band. Starting a band isn't anything spectacular as I've been in several squadron bands myself. The amazing thing about this band, however, is that *every* song they sang was original. The band, called the *Eight Balls*, performed for us one night at a reunion dinner. I will never forget how everyone in that room bonded together.

Those weren't *their* songs; they were *our* songs! They were fighter pilot songs! They weren't the remanufactured songs we sing today handed down by rugby teams; these were original songs about what it means to be a fighter pilot! They were songs about defending the skies over the White Sands (the airspace practically in our own backyard) and how they struggled with many of the same problems we struggle with today: weather cancellations, maintenance ground aborts, rogue red air, constant deployments, and airborne buffoonery. These songs had meaning and depth.

At the end of the reunion, the last song of the night was the *Whiffenpoof Song* — the only song sung that night without fighter pilot origin. The song, although not our own, has deep meaning to the Black Sheep. The song was written in 1909 and was the standard closing piece of the Whiffenpoofs—a men's a cappella group at Yale. The song was adopted as the squadron song circa the Korean War. The song's haunting melody and sincere words remind us how singing brings us together as a band of brothers—a true fraternity:

## The Whiffenpoof Song

> To the tables down at Mory's,
> To the place where Louis dwells,
> To the dear old Temple Bar
> We love so well,
>
>
> Sing the Whiffenpoofs assembled
> With their glasses raised on high,
> And the magic of their singing casts its spell.
>
> Yes, the magic of their singing
> Of the songs we love so well:
> Shaliwasting and Mavourneen and the rest.
> We will serenade our Louis
> While life and voice shall last
> Then we'll pass and be forgotten with the rest.
>
> We are poor little lambs
> Who have lost our way.
> Baa! Baa! Baa!
> We are little **Black Sheep**
> Who have gone astray.

*Baa! Baa! Baa!*
*Gentlemen songsters off on a spree*
*Damned from here to eternity*
*God have mercy on such as we.*
*Baa! Baa! Baa!*

*This* was why we started singing songs! A true fighter pilot song laments our plight: that we strive for glory, we fight hard, and when we die we are forgotten! A real fighter pilot song unites the squadron, as demonstrated by the Black Sheep of yesteryear. On my ride home from the reunion that night, I pondered the stark contrast between the fighter pilot songs of yore and those we sing today.

The songs presently sung in the fighter squadron bar are meant to be more lighthearted. They are intended to help us forget our dwindling numbers, declining budgets, and aging technology. Although fighter pilot songs have always been well-intentioned, their nature has changed significantly from the days of singing songs like the *Whiffenpoof Song*.

In today's politically-correct climate, the fighter pilot bar is being forced to make a return to its origins. Many songs we have sung over the past two decades have now been deemed off-limits by superiors. Commanders have been counseled to rein in their squadron members and ensure they act professionally both on duty and off. While it is sad to see the end of an era of tradition, it is an opportunity for today's fighter pilots to establish new ones. It's an opportunity to take the time and write fighter pilot songs that we may claim as our own. Songs you won't find random people singing in some dive bar.

## The Greats

Although many great songs echo in the rafters of the squadron bar, some have withstood the test of time better than others. Granted, the titles and lyrics to many of these songs are so offensive they could make Lil Wayne blush. One of the greatest songs that can be reproduced in this forum (i.e. Rated PG-13) is a song that every fighter pilot knows.

*Dear Mom* was originally written in 1941, inspired by the Selective Service Act of 1940. It was simply a letter from a deployed serviceman to his mother. Once the fighter pilot community got hold of it during the Vietnam War, it was changed to reflect the plight of an OV-10 Bronco pilot. Bronco pilots were used as Forward Air Controllers (FACs) at the time and had limited firepower with which to defend themselves. The song has since been modified over the years as an ode to combat pilots everywhere.

One of two versions of the song is sung in fighter squadrons today. The version I cite here was modified in the Vietnam War Era (*The Bronco Song* shown below.) Another version of the song was modified during Desert Storm. Here is the most widely sung version of the song:

## Dear Mom... (aka *The Bronco Song*)

> *Dear Mom, your son is dead, he bought the farm today*

*He crashed his OV-10 on Ho Chi Min's*
*highway*
*It was a rocket pass, and then he busted his*
*ass,*
*Mmm, mmm, mmm*

*He went across the fence to see what he*
*could see*
*And there it was as plain as it could be,*
*It was a truck on the road, with a big heavy*
*load,*
*Mmm, mmm, mmm*

*He got right on the horn and gave the*
*DASC a call*
*"Send me air, I've got a truck that's*
*stalled!"*
*The DASC said, "That's all right, I'll send*
*you BLACK SHEEP Flight"*
*(Insert your squadron mascot)*
*For I am the power!*

*The fighters checked right in, gunfighters*
*two by two*
*Low on gas and tanker overdue*
*They asked the FAC to mark just where*
*that truck was parked,*
*Mmm, mmm, mmm*

*The FAC he rolled right in with his smoke*
*to mark*
*Exactly where that truck was parked*
*And the rest is in doubt because he never*
*pulled out,*
*Mmm, mmm, mmm*

*(On one knee with reverence)*

*Dear Mom your son is dead, he bought the
farm today,
He crashed his OV-10 on Ho Chi Min's
highway
It was a rocket pass and then he busted his
ass,
Mmm, mmm, mmm*

*Him! Him! **** Him!
How did he go? Straight in!
What was he doing? 169!
Indicated? Calibrated?
True! (Reference to Indicated Airspeed,
Calibrated Airspeed, and True Airspeed.)*

Another popular song brought out during Roll
Call isn't really a song at all. *Counting to Ten* is more of an
exercise — mental gymnastics, if you will — that proves
humorous in a room mostly full of intoxicated fighter
pilots. *Counting to Ten* (also known as *One Hen, Two
Ducks,* or simply *The Announcer's Test*) took root in the
early 1940s as a radio announcer's test given at Radio
Central New York. The test was administered to
prospective announcers to ascertain their memory,
enunciation, and diction and to determine their
worthiness to go "on air."

The person leading the exercise counts to ten as
shown below, with the others in the room echoing the
words after the leader recites them. When one line is
completed, the leader starts at the top of the list and
recites the cumulative list through to the next number
(e.g. "One hen. One hen, two ducks. One hen, two ducks,
three squawking geese..." and so on.) The faster the

person leading the exercise can recite it, the funnier the results. Try to keep up.

## Counting to Ten

*One* hen.

*Two* ducks.

*Three* squawking geese.

*Four* limerick oysters.

*Five* corpulent porpoises

*Six* pairs of Don Alverzo's tweezers.

*Seven* thousand Macedonians in full battle array.*

(*This section is often modified as "dressed in full battle armor.")

*Eight* brass monkeys from the ancient, sacred crypts of Egypt.

*Nine* apathetic, sympathetic, diabetic old men on roller skates with a marked propensity towards procrastination and sloth.

*Ten* lyrical, spherical, diabolical denizens of the deep who all stall around the corner of the quo, the quay, and the quivery, all at the same time.

No one knows when the *Announcer's Test* made its way into the fighter squadron, but it has since served to test the skills of inebriated fighter pilots everywhere.

As mentioned earlier, songs are not only sung for fun but can help the squadron deal with tragedy. Many songs are found in squadron song books that help the group deal with losses, should they occur. They are typically sung reverently and followed by a moment of silence if sung for a departed fighter pilot. One such song is *Blue Four*.

## Blue Four

*There's a fireball down there on the hillside,*
*And I think maybe we've lost a friend,*
*But we'll keep on flying, and we'll keep on dying,*
*For duty and honor never end.*

*There's an upended glass on the table,*
*Down in front a lone, empty chair.*
*Yesterday we were with him, today God be with him,*
*Wherever he is in your care.*

*They were four when they took off this morning,*
*And their duty was there in the sky.*
*Only three ships returning, Blue Four ain't returning,*
*To Blue Four hold your glasses high.*

*There's a fireball down there on the
hillside,
And I think maybe we've lost a friend,
But we'll keep on flying, and we'll keep on
dying,
For duty and honor never end.*

## Other Popular Fighter Pilot Songs

The quantity of songs in the fighter pilot's repertoire approaches the hundreds. While not every fighter pilot is familiar with every song, usually everyone joins in the singing at some point. Here are the titles of some fighter pilot favorites that are widely known throughout the Air Force. The list is certainly not comprehensive, but should prove to give the promising young fighter pilot a good starting point. The lyrics aren't provided here, but a quick online search should turn them up for you.

*Adeline Schmidt*

*Along a Northeast Railroad*

*Baby Seal Song*

*Fox One in the Face*

*I Don't Want to Join the Air Force*

*I Love My Wife*

*I Used to Work in Chicago*

*Is Everybody Happy?*

*Mary Ann Burns*

*Music Man*

*Sammy Small*

*Throw a Nickel on the Grass*

In many ways, music is a coping mechanism for the fighter pilot. Many of us have lost friends in the business. Training accidents and combat fatalities are a reality for every fighter pilot. Singing is a way to get your mind off the heavy stuff and let out some of the frustration. Regardless of limitations placed on lyrical enjoyment by commanding officers, fighter pilot songs will forever be sung by fighter pilots. They are part of our heritage!

Oh… and if anyone ever asks you who Mary Ann Burns was, just smile and tell them she was the queen of all the acrobats. (Mom, do NOT look this one up.)

# Fighter Pilot Games

Competition is a critical part of a fighter pilot's life. Without it, we would wither and die. Fighter pilots play games for one reason, and one reason only: to show you how much better we are than everyone else! We never lose, except when we do. When that happens, you can bet we will go double or nothing!

Some games are more worthy of a fighter pilot's time than others. Games deserving of a fighter pilot's attention typically have two things in common: 1) they involve a monetary increase for the winner and 2) they provide an opportunity for someone (the player or the player's stunt drinker) to imbibe an adult beverage. As with everything a fighter pilot does, it's better to be lucky than good, but being good helps!

### A Gentleman's Game

I'd been a student flying the mighty T-38C for nearly two months when my flight commander informed us that we were having a flight get-together to blow off steam and relax from the rigors of pilot training. The party involved the members of my class and five other student pilots in our flight who made up our upper class. To say there had been animosity between our classes would be an understatement. One member of our upper class, who we called "Lurch" due to his tall, muscle-less frame and horrible attitude, had been a particular thorn in our side.

Our upper class took every opportunity to derail us and make us look like a bunch of buffoons in front of our flight commander while they sucked up to him. I wasn't sure how this social evening would pan out given the delicate state of politics between our two classes in the flight.

The formal portion of the evening's activities ended uneventfully, and we all proceeded to the Officer's Club for a gentleman's game of CRUD. It was the first time many of us had played the game. CRUD is a full-contact sport played on a snooker table (more to follow on CRUD), and my class looked forward to putting a hurt on the upper-class weenies. After the rules were explained to us, we split into two teams: Team Upper Class and Team Lower Class.

The game kicked off as we each took turns going one on one against the members of our upper class. I looked at the lineup on the board and couldn't help but smile when I saw that I would be competing against Lurch. My rotation finally came around as I became the Shooter. My object was to roll the cue ball with my hand to knock the only other ball on the table, a striped pool ball, into one of the corner pockets at the opposite end of the table. Lurch's objective was to keep me from achieving mine.

Before I could take a shot, I had to get to the cue ball. Lurch positioned himself between me and the cue ball rolling slowly to the end of the table opposite me. In blatant violation of the rules, Lurch held on to the side of the table to better fortify his position.

I wasn't even thinking about the cue ball as I lowered my shoulder and sped towards the gangly turd in a flight suit. The look in his eye indicated his confidence in his ability to keep me from reaching my objective. I impacted Lurch at full speed, who was thrown, surprisingly easily, from his dug-in position at the side of the table.

All eyes were on the six-foot-something student pilot as he took to the skies in the O'Club as a result of my hit. It was almost like watching a movie in slow motion as this human projectile hurled through the air and landed on a nearby table, sending half-empty glasses and plates of devoured chicken wings flying.

We all looked at the Judge (the ref in the game of CRUD) to see who would be assessed a life: him for breaking the rules, or me for getting him airborne. The Judge's decision to assess a life on Lurch was accompanied by cheers from my classmates. We hadn't won the game yet, but it felt like we had just gained a major victory.

I don't remember who won that round, or any of the multiple rounds that were played late into the night. After we took our aggressions out on Lurch, the mood between classes lightened. We spent the remainder of the evening living like the fighter pilots we hoped to become upon graduation.

Fighter pilot games are an integral part of life in a fighter squadron. What follows is a list of some of the favorite games you will see played in fighter bars around the Air Force. The list is not all-inclusive, and the descriptions are not intended to be a complete set of rules, rather an overview of how the games are played. Each squadron adds, subtracts, or changes rules as required to tailor the game to the unit.

## CRUD

This game is a fighter pilot staple and is often viewed as the pinnacle of games requiring athletic prowess and cunning skill. Its origins are with the Canadian Air Force. (This makes up for Canada giving us Tom Green.) People have gone to the hospital with broken bones, ligament tears, and concussions from playing CRUD.

Make no mistake; this is a full contact sport and not for the faint of heart. It is typically only played in the squadron bar or at the club on base. Civilian for-profit establishments just aren't equipped to handle a group of rowdy fighter pilots diving over tables, breaking glasses, beating each other down, and scaring off other patrons.

CRUD is a game with a lot of rules, and I mean a *lot* of rules. Here's the gist of the game.

*Objective of the Game:* Eliminate all three "lives" of each player on the opposite team by any means necessary.

*Required Items:* A snooker table (primary) or pool table (secondary), a cue ball (known as the "Shooter Ball") and a striped ball (known as the "Object Ball"), two teams of exceptionally rambunctious fighter pilots, a Judge (a.k.a Ref or Crudmeister), and score keeper (optional.)

*How It's Played:* Two teams are formed. The names of each player are listed by team on a chalkboard with sufficient space to the right of the name for three large Xs (each to be added when a player loses a life.) The Judge obtains a beverage (imperative for assessing safety violations) and positions himself at the center of a table. Before the game commences, a starting team is determined by the "lag."

*The Lag:* The Lag is the equivalent of the coin toss before a football game. The captains of each CRUD team stand side by side at one end of the CRUD table (designated as the "Shooter" end.) Each simultaneously rolls a ball (both the Shooter Ball and Object Ball are used) to the opposite end of the table in an attempt to bounce it off the opposite end and have it return without touching the sides. The team whose ball returns closest to the Shooter end without touching it gets to choose whether they serve or receive to open the round.

*The Serve:* The Object Ball is placed six inches from the receiver end of the table and centered between sides. The Shooter is given three attempts to hit the Object Ball by any means necessary to include bumping it off the sides. If the Object Ball is not hit within three attempts, the Shooter loses a life, and the serve is turned over to the next team. The Defender may not touch either the Shooter Ball or the Object Ball at any point. Once the Object Ball is struck, the Defender becomes the Shooter and the next player in line on the serving team becomes the Defender with the previous Shooter exiting the playing area.

*The Shooter:* Once the Object Ball is in play, the Shooter must keep it moving by striking it with the Shooter ball. The Shooter may only take shots from the short ends of the table defined as being in between imaginary 45-degree lines extending outward from each corner. If the Object Ball ceases to move at any time, a "dead ball" is called by the judge and the Shooter loses a life. If the Shooter manages to sink the Object Ball into a corner pocket, the Defender (either the current Defender or previous depending upon the call of the judge) is the one to lose a life.

*The Defender:* Defenders are not allowed to touch any ball in play. There are limited rules for blocking, and discretion is left to the judge as to what level of physical contact is allowed for a Defender to block a Shooter from taking a shot. Aside from the permissible contact with the Shooter, a Defender may use any means necessary to delay, deceive, or distract the Shooter to prevent him from sinking the object the ball.

*The Rules:* A full list of official CRUD rules was compiled by the American CRUD Players Association (ACPA) in the year 2000. The rules have been circulating around the internet and do not have a permanent home. You may download the ACPA's Official Rules by visiting: **http://www.pianoburning.com/wp-content/uploads/2016/12/ACPA-Official-Crud-Rules-2000.pdf**

Any violation of the rules will result in a ruling by the judge as to whether the violator is assessed a life.

*The Judge:* Physical contact with the Judge is prohibited during the game. Should the Judge spill his drink due to contact with a player, the Judge will assess a life on that player, and depending on the heinousness of the contact, may assess multiple lives. Quibbling is not allowed, but spirited argument may be undertaken by the captain of the CRUD team in question. If the Judge rules the argument to be unfounded or just plain off-the-wall ridiculous, a life may be assessed on the team captain. Bottom line, don't mess with the Judge or suck up to the Judge unless you're a bystander. Then you can throw all the spears you want!

At the end of the day, CRUD is a game intended to allow players to both establish dominance and strengthen brotherhood. If we were heathens, we would walk on hot coals, but since we're not, we play CRUD.

## Dollar Bill Game

This game is a variation of the bar game called *Liar's Dice*. The Dollar Bill Game, as played in the fighter squadron bar, is a game of deception, educated guessing, skill, and pure fighter pilot luck.

*Objective of the Game:* Do **not** guess the numbers in the specified position of the dollar bill's serial number.

*Required Items:* A single U.S. Dollar Bill. (AMERICA!)

*How It's Played:* The player starting off is considered the holder of the "hammer" and is referred to as "The Hammer." The Hammer may be selected in any fashion, but is either the person who instigated the game, or the loser of the previous Dollar Bill Game (be sure to keep adequate records if a significant amount of time elapses between games!) The holder of the hammer sets the game in motion.

1) Players form a circle and charge their glasses. The charging of the glasses is purely administrative at this point.
2) The Hammer pulls a dollar bill out of his or her wallet without allowing others in the circle to see the bill's serial number.
3) The Hammer asks the person on his/her right to declare "first two" or "last two." This phraseology specifies the position of the numbers to be used in the bill's serial number. The number now becomes "the objective."
4) The Hammer now beings play by asking the person to his/her left to guess a number between 0-99. The guesser hopes

and prays the number guessed is not the objective!

5) The Hammer will declare whether the guess is high or low and the turn now passes to the next person in the circle away from the Hammer.

6) The next person to guess attempts to establish a bracket around the objective. If the Hammer said the previous guess was low, the next guesser then picks a higher number to establish an upper bound to the guesses that are to follow.

7) As each person in the circle guesses, they try to close the bracket in as close to the objective as possible without actually guessing the objective.

8) If the objective is guessed at any point, that person loses and buys a round for the table.

9) The Hammer may apply deception to target a certain individual or to create chaos and confusion in the group. If the loser suspects deception is in play, he/she may challenge the Hammer. If the Hammer loses the challenge, then the Hammer buys the round. If no deception was applied in the round and the objective was guessed, the challenger pays double.

*Combat rules* may be applied to limit the amount of buffoonery or maximize the beverage intake (this is especially useful late in the evening to take advantage of those in a deeper state of inebriation than others.)

1) Combat rules must be established before starting the game and are upheld regardless of the quibbling or complaining that is sure to ensue.
2) "First two" or "last two" is established before the bill is viewed.
3) The Hammer takes only one look at the bill then lays it face down on the table.
4) If the Hammer forgets the object, he buys a round.
5) If any player asks what the bracket currently is, that player buys a round.
6) If any player guesses outside the bracket, they purchase a round.

This game may be played comm-out (silent) using only hand signals. Comm-out visual signals are not established prior to starting the game and all combat rules apply.

## 4-5-6

This little dice game can immediately catapult you to instant fame and fortune or break you and destroy your marriage. The game is based on an old Chinese game of chance and has many variations. Be sure to understand which set of rules are in play before putting your money on the table.

*Objective of the Game:* Simple — take your bros' money.

*Items Needed:* Three dice and a wad of cash (preferably in denominations of $1 unless you want the game to end quickly.)

*How It's Played:* As with the dollar bill game, a holder of the "hammer" is nominated. The player holding the hammer may lose it under certain circumstances (to be explained shortly.) If the hammer is lost, it passes to the next player on the left of the original Hammer. Circumstances that cause the current holder of the hammer to lose it:

1) If all of the players beat the Hammer in a given round.
2) A player rolls 4 - 5 - 6 in a single turn.
3) A player rolls triples.

Before commencing play, the Hammer establishes the initial bet, known as the "pot," by throwing cash down in the middle of the table. Once the hammer has set the pot, it is up to the other players to either "cover" or "fade" the pot. By covering the pot, all players' bets match the amount of the initial bet. If a player doesn't want to cover the pot, they can fade the pot by an amount they can or want to bet. If this happens, other players may increase their bets to collectively cover the pot. If the pot is not covered, the hammer removes the excess of the initial bet from the pot.

Regardless of whether the pot is covered or faded, once betting is complete, the Hammer says, "Pot's Right!" and the last person to bet tells the Hammer, "Shoot 'em!"

*The Hammer rolls the dice.* There are four outcomes of the Hammer's roll of the dice.

1) **Automatic Win.** If the Hammer rolls a 4 - 5 - 6, triples, or a pair of non-6s with a 6 (e.g. 2 - 2 - 6), the Hammer instantly wins all bets.

2) **Automatic Loss.** If the Hammer rolls a 1 - 2 - 3 or a pair of non-1s with a 1 (e.g. 6 - 6 - 1), the Hammer instantly loses all bets.

3) **Set Point.** If the Hammer rolls a pair with a third number between 1 and 6 (e.g. 4 - 4 - 2), the third number becomes the set point. This will be the number for the others to beat.

4) **Re-roll.** If none of the above conditions are met, the Hammer continues to roll until getting an automatic win or loss, or setting a point.

With a point set, the rest of the players take turns rolling. Each player's roll will have one of three outcomes:

1) **Automatic Win.** If the player rolls a 4 - 5 - 6, triples, a pair of non-6s with a 6, or a pair and point higher than the set point (e.g. The Hammer set a point of 3, and the

71

player rolls a 2 - 2 - 4), the player picks up the hammer for the next round.

2) **Automatic Loss.** If the player rolls a 1 - 2 - 3, a pair of non-1s with a 1 (e.g. 6 - 6 -1), or a pair and a point less than the set point (e.g. The Hammer set a point of 3, and the player rolls a 5 - 5 - 2), the player loses and is out of the round. His bet stays in the pot and is awarded to the winner of the round.

3) **Push.** If player rolls a pair and a number equal to the set point (e.g. Hammer set a point of 3, and the player rolls a 4 - 4 -3.), no money is exchanged and play moves to the next player.

4) **Re-roll.** No automatic win or loss is rolled.

Variations to these rules can be made to make the game more or less complicated. Some fighter squadrons use 4 - 5 - 6 as the only automatic win or only allow you to pull money from the pot if you hit this magical combination. Again, be sure you understand what rules are in play before the hostilities begin!

### Fighter Pilot Luck

Fighter pilots make their own luck. Cicero quoted an old proverb in the 1st Century BCE: "Fortune favors the bold." Since then, warriors everywhere have adopted it as their mantra. In combat, we are prepared, know the ROE, and fight with the determination of Spartacus. We take a similar approach in the gaming arena. Fighter pilots understand that things don't just happen for a reason. Instead, we believe that we drive the fight. Take this attitude into your next game and enjoy the spoils of war!

# The Legend of Jeremiah Weed

The F-4 Phantom, still somewhat heavy with a full fuel load, started its break turn into the bandit. It was a wintery morning in 1978 over the Nevada Test and Training Range (NTTR), and the azure sky was utterly void of clouds — it was the perfect day for a fight! The pilot in the front seat of the Phantom twisted his body to look back towards the tail of his jet as he tried to maintain sight of the enemy aircraft. With his attention drawn aft of the aircraft, he didn't notice the glowing red light indicating a fire in the right engine. Although he didn't see the light, he soon saw the smoke trailing his aircraft as the fight matured over the barren desert floor below.

"Knock it off! Knock it off!"

The radio call from the crippled jet was echoed by his wingman, and signaled the end of the training engagement. With his attention now turned to the engine gauges of the Vietnam-Era fighter, the Phantom pilot assessed the situation. The right engine had to be shut down immediately. The pilot in the back seat, a fellow Phantom driver who couldn't stand to see a cockpit go empty, had only wanted to get airborne on a day he wasn't scheduled to fly. Now, the back seater was helping the front seater work through the checklist to recover the aircraft back to Nellis Air Force Base.

With the engine shut down, the aircrew reassessed the fire situation. The crippled jet was losing fuel fast; the fire must have ruptured fuel lines to the good engine. Not only were they losing fuel, but the operating engine now began to wheeze and cough. The duo had no choice; it was time to give the jet back to the taxpayers.

With no more time to reference checklists, the two pilots accomplished the ejection procedures by memory. Each pilot assumed the proper posture in his seat in preparation for the violent expulsion from the aircraft. The front seat pilot gave the command to bail out, and in a matter of seconds, the two aviators were dangling beneath their respective parachute canopies. Their speedy recovery now depended almost entirely on their wingman who witnessed their ejection as he began directing rescue efforts for the two unlucky pilots.

As the pilots dangled in their chutes, they watched their crippled F-4 hit the ground in a cloud of dirt, debris, and fire. By the time the rescue forces arrived, the jet was a smoking hole in the earth.

In December of 1979, one year after the crash, the two pilots were reunited—this time as F-16 pilots having transitioned to the new airframe after the incident in the F-4. The two pilots met in the O'Club bar and reminisced over the experience of bailing out of their burning fighter jet. As the night wore on, they became determined to revisit the crash site and camp out in the crater made by their doomed Phantom.

The following morning, they took one of their bros, rented a car and some camping gear, and headed out into the Nevada desert. All they had to go on were rough coordinates noted on maps they sketched the previous day while flying over the site in their Vipers. Without a precise location, they searched for hours trying to find the impact area. The sun was setting by the time they reached the general area of the crash site, and the increasing darkness made navigation nearly impossible. They decided to turn back to a small bar they had passed several miles back and come up with a new plan.

The three fighter pilots entered the ramshackle little bar — the only habitation for miles around — to find the bar occupied only by a bearded bartender and an elderly patron passed out at a table in the corner. As one would expect from a small bar in such an isolated location, the liquor supply was limited. In a matter of hours, the aviators had consumed the bulk of the stock. With nothing better to do, one of the pilots suggested they play a game of Afterburner.

Afterburner is a drinking game wherein flame is applied to a shot of liquor, lighting the top layer of the beverage on fire. The object is to consume the drink without burning your body or anything attached to it. The bartender indicated that while his alcohol supply was all but exhausted, he thought he might have something that would work. The bewhiskered man disappeared behind a curtain over a crumbling door frame and re-emerged triumphantly with three bottles of a substance foreign to the fighter pilots.

"This here, gentlemen, is Jeremiah Weed. It's a bourbon that should suit your little game just fine," said the grizzly old barkeep as he produced four shot glasses before his customers — the fourth being for himself.

The three glasses in front of the pilots were lit and, in true fighter pilot fashion, were downed without a hitch leaving a small blue flame at the bottom of each glass.

The bartender poured himself a shot, and one of the pilots lit it. The bearded patron hesitated for several seconds as he stroked his beard away from his mouth — a critical mistake. Those few key moments allowed the flame to heat the rim of the shot glass to a dangerous temperature. The man threw the shot back, flinching as the heated glass seared his lips. A small flinch was all it took for the fire in the glass to spread to his beard.

The bartender screamed in pain as he dove toward the sink. The fighter pilots sprung to the aid of the barkeeper, extinguishing the flame. But it was too late. The bartender had lost a sizable portion of beard, and the smell of burning hair and flesh permeated the air. The commotion had woken the old man passed out in the corner who now joined the group to find out what happened.

After repeated heartfelt apologies from the instigators of the game, the old man asked the three strangers what they were doing in this neck of the woods. The pilots felt obliged to spill the beans on their mission to find the F-4's crash site. Lucky for them, the old man knew exactly where it was and offered to take them to it.

Still feeling sorry for the situation with the bartender, the fighter pilots purchased the two remaining bottles of Jeremiah Weed and left the now partially bearded barkeeper a substantial tip before heading out the door.

With the help of the mysterious bar patron, the fighter pilots easily found the crash site and spent the cold December night in the crater drinking both of the recently procured bottles of "Weed."

Upon returning from their desert adventure, the pilots took one of the empty bottles of Jeremiah Weed to the O'Club. They presented it to the manager and demanded he stock it in the bar. The manager had never heard of the beverage, but after some searching acquired several bottles for the Club.

Today, hundreds of fighter pilots from around the world converge at the Nellis O'Club every year for an exercise called *Red Flag*. Friday nights at the club are spent in typical fighter pilot fashion, and fighter pilot traditions from the various countries represented are shared and enjoyed. The traditions may change from time to time, but the one constant in the Nellis O'Club, and in every fighter pilot bar in America, is the presence of Jeremiah Weed.

In 1980, the three fighter pilot friends rejoined once again at Nellis with the intent of revisiting the crash site and the little hole-in-the-wall bar where they had spent such an eventful evening. Upon reaching the location of the bar, they found nothing but desert. In fact, there was no sign of a bar — or any edifice for that matter — ever having been established at that location. The fighter pilots tried to figure out if it had all been just a dream. They came to the conclusion that their encounter with the bartender and Jeremiah Weed that fateful night must have been a gift from the Gods. For that reason, Jeremiah Weed is often referred to in fighter pilot bars as "The Nectar of the Gods."

## Significance

This tradition is one that is specific to the United States Air Force. As such, it is highly regarded and held as sacred amongst fighter pilots. This legend is retold to young wingmen when they are given a call sign during their naming ceremonies. Younger generations of pilots are expected to pass it on when they become the ones running the ceremonies.

The details of the Legend of Jeremiah Weed vary. Although the legend has been modified slightly over the years thanks to the *10% Rule*, it will forever remain an important piece of American fighter pilot heritage.

# The Tactical Call Sign

"I want you to climb above the contrails, push it up to Mach 1.5, shoot everything, and don't turn around — let the second wave pick up the leakers."

Those were the words from my Ops Group Commander — who happened to be the overall commander for this installment of Exercise Red Flag — as he shared his expectations with my squadron's contingent of fighter pilots.

It was my first sortie as a mission qualified F-22 wingman, and I was eager to prove my worth as a fighter pilot. I was number four in the first of two four-ships that would be protecting a strike train consisting of A-10s, B-52s, and British Harriers. Due to the relatively slow speeds of the strikers, they would require a longer window of protection getting to and from the target area. To make matters worse, we were expecting at least a 5:1 ratio of Red Air to Blue Air Escort, which meant that every missile we carried would count.

We took off into the radiant Nevada morning and pointed the noses of our Raptors towards the tanker track. In a matter of minutes, we rejoined with our designated refueler, a KC-135, and topped off our fuel tanks before proceeding to the marshaling area in preparation for the fight.

The radios were relatively silent as the *fight's on* time approached. Minutes before the fight was to begin, Air Battle Managers aboard the AWACS began describing the airborne threats in the airspace. The "picture" was given over the radio in bullseye format (bearing and range from a known point) and consisted of so many bandits I lost track.

My flight lead began doling out targeting responsibilities to the members of our flight. As he was doing so, I heard heavy static on the radio frequency and something that sounded like someone playing an organ. The enemy was attempting to jam our communications. It was a lot for a young wingman to process. Nevertheless, I was determined to target my group and kill every contact in it.

I went to work digging through the mess of tracks showing up on my displays. I worked feverishly to find my targets and stay on my intercept timeline. I finally got everything figured out (or so I thought), and it was time to start shooting.

"Rocket four, fox three, four-ship, South group, heavy, four contacts," I practically screamed on the radio. I was so proud of myself. I had missiles inbound to the leading edge of enemy aircraft, and I was about to be a hero! A little more than a minute had passed, but my missiles hadn't yet impacted their targets—in fact, they still had about a minute to go. Weird. And why hadn't anyone else called their missile shots yet? It was about this time I noticed all my targets turning cold (180 degrees of turn away from me.)

"Rocket 4, kill South group, four contacts, thirty-six thousand stack sixteen thousand." I was almost smiling as I called my first Red Flag kills. It was shortly after that I heard my flight mates calling their first shots. I dismissed the giant question mark in my mind and continued to fight.

With the bulk of Red Air destroyed, the strikers pushed out from the marshaling area. Now that we had sanitized the airspace, they had unimpeded runs to their targets. We quickly established our reset CAPs as we held above the target area to protect the vulnerable strikers.

I did a quick weapons inventory to find that I only had two medium-range missiles left. I wouldn't be able to shoot more than two bandits beyond visual range (BVR.) I found myself wishing I hadn't shot as many missiles at the first wave of bandits.

As the enemy fighters regenerated, it was only a matter of time before I was completely out of missiles and of no use to the strikers below. With disgust in his voice, Rocket One—my flight lead—cleared me to return to Nellis. Keeping me in the fight without missiles would mean having one more aircraft to escort. I returned home wondering how I could have conserved my weapons better.

Back on the ground, I reviewed my tapes and validated my shots. It was then that I noticed the range at which I took my initial shots. Why didn't I see it airborne? I had shot long, *very* long, and the drag maneuver the bandits executed defeated all the shots on which I had called kills. I was feeling a little sheepish. My first shots at Red Flag were all defeated because I didn't have the awareness I thought I had.

To make matters worse, I had to stand up in the air-to-air shot evaluation in front of a hundred other pilots and explain why I had called invalid kills on the radio resulting in four of the bandits kill removing. Such a heinous crime would cost me $5 per bandit paid to Red Air in accordance with fighter pilot tradition.

Unfortunately, the story doesn't end with the $5 penalty. The story would come back to haunt me exactly six months later at my naming ceremony.

A fighter pilot naming ceremony is one of the holiest of fighter pilot traditions. During the ceremony, stories are told about the young fighter pilot being named, and jokes are made to initiate the new pilot into the "brotherhood." Initiation is complete when The Benevolent Naming Committee — consisting of all the named fighter pilots in the squadron — have given the newbie a tactical name. No longer will the rookie be known by his or her own name or by a generic one used for new squadron members (e.g. *Nitz, FNG, Bogan,* etc.)

From that moment on, the new fighter pilot is known by the name they received during the ceremony.

## Origins of the Call Sign

No one knows exactly where the concept of the call sign was conceived. According to U.S. Air Force Historian Yvonne Kincaid, the use of tactical names probably originated during the early part of World War II. The first call signs were likely used by ground controllers to communicate with pilots, as air-to-air radio communication wasn't efficient at that time. It was faster and easier to call a pilot by his nickname. The use of a call sign provided an added benefit— it limited the ability of the enemy to gather intelligence on friendly pilots by listening to un-secure frequencies.

Since those early days, call signs have become a sacred tradition in the military flying community. You don't come up with your own call sign; you must receive it from the Naming Committee. Names are given based on the commission of a heinous act, can be associated with a physical characteristic of the person being named, or are based on a natural play off the person's name.

My call sign was given to me at a meticulously planned (and questionably executed) naming ceremony. The nature of the naming ceremony is holy to the fighter pilot community, so I won't go into too much detail. But like Roll Call, the naming ceremony follows an agenda. Usually, the Weapons Officer runs the naming as it is considered a tactical rite, but that role may be delegated to the Mayor if required. My squadron's Patch was the one in charge of my naming ceremony because I was the Mayor in the squadron at the time.

The air was thick with anticipation as I was ushered in before The Benevolent Naming Committee. They had been deliberating for what seemed like an eternity on what to name me. I was shown the list of names, none of which were very good. I cringed when I saw the name *Choch Face* on the list.

A week before the ceremony, some of the older guys in the squadron took pity on me and explained the naming process. They underscored the importance of providing a bribe to the Naming Committee in hopes they would smile down upon me and grant me a good name. One of the other un-named wingmen and I had taken upon ourselves the task of renovating the Heritage Room and personally stocking it with beverages we knew would appeal to those in charge of naming us.

After some deliberation in my presence, the Patch kicked me out of the room for some closed-door deliberation. When I returned, the list had been narrowed down to *Choch Face* and *Demon*, the mascot of our sister squadron. I began to sweat as I contemplated the results of either name. On the one hand, I would have to live with a humiliating call sign that didn't make any sense. On the other, I would go forward appearing as a traitor to the Black Sheep. If asked, I was determined not to be a Benedict Arnold. I would endure a life of humiliation, if necessary, to not betray my squadron.

Just as I anticipated, the Patch asked me what I wanted to be named, and true to my composition, I went with *Choch Face*. I was kicked out of the room once again to the sound of uncontrollable laughter. My stomach turned as I waited alone to see if the Benevolent Naming Committee would ratify the horrific call sign.

I stood up straight as I was brought before the group for the final verdict. My back was to the chalkboard upon which was written my destiny. The laughter from my last appearance was just beginning to die down. I could barely keep my composure as I knew I was about to see the name by which I would be known for the rest of my career.

"Alright, Choch Face, turn around and look at the board," said the Patch.

I closed my eyes and pivoted 180 degrees. Relief washed over me like a crashing wave when I opened my eyes to see the name *Shotz* written on the board. My Red Flag antics had been name-worthy. Either that, or they must have liked my bribe.

## Sample Call Signs

Here is a smattering of call sign stories I've heard in no particular order. Most are based upon a heinous act, but as you can see, fighter pilots are given whatever nickname seems to fit them the best.

**TROJAN** — Took a corner taxiing too fast at night, and his nose wheel tire departed the rim. In other words, his Tire Rolled Off the Jet At Night.

**Splash** — This infamous bandit-slayer was on a banzai intercept in the simulator while his flight lead had just exited from a potential merge and was running cold. The soon-to-be-named fighter pilot told his flight lead "Splash Two" at the location of his flight lead's shots, indicating the bandits he was targeting were dead. Believing the threat had been eliminated and it was safe for him to turn around and continue on flow, the flight lead recommitted. As soon as the flight lead turned around, he took a heater to the face from a live bandit and died. In other words, "Splash Two" was really "Splash One" as the other bandit had lived!

**TULSA** — Total Utter Lack of Situational Awareness

**Clothsoff** — Last name "Oliver."

**Elmer** — The "mishap" pilot was golfing with the bros when one of his drives hit a rabbit, nearly taking its cranium off. He assessed a clean kill on the rabbit, and the bros determined he was a regular *Elmer Fudd*.

**Buzz** — This freshly minted pilot hit a buzzard circling over the approach end of the runway. The bird impacted just outboard of the engine nacelle resulting in only small damage to the aircraft, and a life-long call sign.

**Rudder** — All thrust, no vector — needs a rudder!

**Jekyll** — Great bro by day, raging intoxicated madman at Roll Call. The Shotmeister is required to keep an eye on this one!

**Jaws** — This poor guy was trapped in the jet when the canopy actuation motor failed. The "jaws of life" were called in to cut him out.

**WreBal** (pronounced "rebel") — Bad things happen to good people. This mild-mannered fighter pilot was driving home from the squadron when he became violently ill. Without warning, he threw up in the passenger seat of his car. The distraction of vomit and tears from retching up the contents of his stomach caused him to run his car through the wall of the base Country Club. He made a fine wrecking ball!

# The Lip Rug

—

*"There's truth and honor in a mustache.*
*And that's why I started flying one on the*
*flagpole outside of my house."*

- **Jarod Kintz**, (The Titanic Would Never
Have Sunk if it Were Made Out of a Sink)

—

## Mustache March

I have a confession to make: I recently bailed on
Mustache March. Yes, I turned my back on this time-
honored tradition in the military flying community — I
shaved my Lip Rug. I have grown several mustaches
throughout my years as a fighter pilot. Historically, I can
count on irritating my wife every March as I unite with
the bros in growing a Flavor Saver, but this year I just
couldn't stick with it. I don't look good with a
"Molestache" (a monster 'stache in its early stages) and
most guys I fly with look ridiculous with one too, but
that's not why I bailed.

I have always enjoyed the unity — the participation with the bros in a combined endeavor — that rolls around each March. Unfortunately, I am not alone in abandoning this annual tradition. Every passing year seems to see record low participation from the fighter community in Mustache March, and I think I know the reason.

Let's digress a moment. If you've ever played on an organized sports team (and I hope you have!), you know how important it is that each player is loyal to the team and dedicated to its success. Psychologists have studied the various social dynamics associated with being part of a team. A lot of money has been spent by professional sports franchises to see to it that their teams perform optimally and with a high degree of cohesion. Team building is more than just a catchphrase — it's a necessity when it comes to optimizing performance. Military teams are no different. They must perform together at a very high level to be effective when the fog and friction of war are present.

So, how do you ensure your team is cohesive and performs well together? That is a question Air Force leaders are continually trying to answer. One former Chief of Staff of the Air Force, General Mark Welsh, tried a novel approach to mitigate the morale crushing effects on the Air Force brought about by force shaping and sequestration. In February 2014, General Welsh extended an invitation to men of every rank and station in the Air Force to join in the tradition of Mustache March. I think his motives were pure and that the invitation to *all* members of the Air Force to participate (either by growing one or by assuming a judging capacity) was good for the overall force. Unfortunately, there were two negative results of this action.

First, it brought out the whiners and complainers. A female Air Force major wrote a scathing article in the Air Force Times about how this mustache competition is just another sign that the military is a "boy's club." It's unfortunate that someone can turn something meant to be lighthearted and fun into an issue of gender discrimination when no bias is present. It is this kind of narrow-minded thinking that is slowly corroding morale amongst the ranks.

According to the Air Force Personnel website, males (aka *mustache growers*) make up 81.1% of the total force. Many units don't even have women in them — not because they aren't allowed, but because statistically there aren't enough females in the force to support this. To be fair, the offended female major may have been subject to discrimination on some level during her career. But to come out in the media with an assault on this upbeat morale builder served only to alienate herself and frustrate others. Unfortunately, because leadership is widely trying to boost morale with an innocent mustache contest, we now have to put up with more whining and complaining.

Second, a broadening of this tradition has made it less unique to fighter pilots in general. By taking a tradition observed by a small group and making it a ritual for everyone, the sacredness of Mustache March has been lost.

## Origins of the 'Stache

The tradition was born when Robin Olds — probably the most revered fighter pilot in USAF history — grew his famous handlebar mustache during the Vietnam War. Colonel Olds fought many battles with the higher-ups on behalf of the men getting slaughtered in the skies. He was tired of losing arguments relating to the lack of information flow and ineffective strategy by those living comfortably on the opposite side of the world from Vietnam. The decision to grow a mustache was made one night in the O'Club and turned into a crusade.

As the "bulletproof" mustache grew, so did its significance in the minds of Colonel Olds and his men. It wasn't meant to be a "middle finger" to leadership in a broad sense (as assumed by the upset major in her article.) Like all of Robin's targeting, the mustache was very precise in its intent. He had lost many battles with leadership in arguments about when and how his men could target the enemy and prosecute their attacks. That was the reason he rebelled, not just for the sake of rebelling. Fighter pilots honor this man for sticking to his guns and doing all he could for his people — even if his only recourse was something as small as growing a mustache.

Growing a mustache every March is not just a way to pay tribute to the legacy of Robin Olds, but more importantly, it solidifies us as a group. According to Social Identity Theory, groups become stronger as they achieve positive distinctiveness. Growing a mustache in March was a way for fighter pilots to distinguish our group from the rest of the masses. I know other groups were honoring this tradition as well, but a requirement from the top extinguishes any distinctiveness we thought we had in honoring this tradition.

Never fear, the mustache will not die. You can't kill awesomeness. The tradition will live on in deployments and may eventually find footing again in the month of March. It will live on in the face of ill-informed naysayers and will continue to be a source of pride for the men who grow them. I will yet again cultivate a mastodonic mustache, but on my own terms, and not at the behest of others. Robin would want it that way. In the end, there is no disputing the fact that mustaches and upper lips were made for each other. Grow one, and you'll see what I mean.

## The Combat 'Stache

If you want to make it home safely from a combat sortie, grow a mustache. If you are unable to grow a mustache, as is the case for most female fighter pilots, you still receive its protective powers by growing one in spirit, whatever that means. The mustache is not just facial hair; it is a frame of mind. It's the cocky, aggressive, slightly ridiculous attitude a combat pilot needs to face his or her foe. It is said that if you ever find yourself deep in the throes of a dogfight, all you must do to win the engagement is drop your oxygen mask. The mustache will do the rest. Oh, and don't forget to give your enemy a courtesy Aim-9 (heat-seeking air-to-air missile) as you do it.

The tradition of the combat mustache was passed on to me while deployed to the Middle East. I had been in the theater for a month and had just gotten through the awkward stage of my mustache growth when word spread through the fighter squadrons that the Ops Group Commander would be inspecting each fighter pilot's mustache to ensure it was within regulations.

One day as I drove to my tent from the flight line, I passed a caravan of 40 some-odd vehicles going the opposite direction. It was the pilots and WSOs (Weapon Systems Officer, pronounced "wiz-oh") of our sister squadron, a squadron of Strike Eagles, on their way in for the inspections. I wondered aloud to the bros in the car with me if they would all trim their mustaches. No self-respecting fighter pilot wants to be regulated in such a manner, and most of us would rather go without a mustache if it came to it. I wouldn't blame the members of the Strike Eagle squadron for shaving it.

The next day I wandered over to our sister squadron to see the fallout. Much to my joy they not only kept their mustaches, but they all shaved their craniums in defiance of such needless oversight! If they were willing to do that just to keep their lip rugs intact, the combat mustache must be important.

Fast forward a couple of years later. I'm back at the same deployed location with another Strike Eagle squadron. A female strike pilot friend of mine had just taken off with her WSO on a combat mission. She missed a critical item on her preflight inspection: her WSO had shaved his mustache! The pair made it uneventfully to their target area, but before dropping any bombs, they were forced to abort the mission for a hydraulic failure. The pair of combat aviators was barely able to safely land at a friendly airfield, albeit not the one they took off from. Was it a coincidence they had such a harrowing experience the day after the WSO shaved his mustache? I think not!

The tradition of the combat mustache mixes purpose and superstition together. We grow the Combat 'Stache in memory of great fighter pilots who grew them before. We keep them while deployed to avoid bad luck.

# The Challenge Coin

Losing money makes you learn a lesson quickly, but it's nothing compared to losing your pride. Unfortunately, I found out that you can learn a lesson by losing both with the tradition of the Challenge Coin. I was appropriately indoctrinated to this tradition during pilot training while going cross-country in the front seat of a T-38C.

We had just taken off as a flight of two with another student and his instructor. My instructor was cooling his heels in the aft cockpit while I was striving to maintain a line-abreast formation with the flight lead. The weather was nice, the radios were quiet, and we had a great weekend ahead of us.

Without warning, my flight lead rocked his wings, signaling his intent for me to rejoin to a close *fingertip* formation.

"Dude," came my instructor's voice over the intercom, "you better get your RMO out."

"My what?" I asked.

"Your Round Metal Object... your coin! He's bringing you in for a coin check!"

I panicked. My recent indoctrination into the Air Force had included a summary of the Challenge Coin tradition, but up to this point, I had yet to experience it. As I closed the distance to within three feet of the lead aircraft, I saw both pilots in the aircraft opposite me holding up their RMOs. They had their oxygen masks lowered and were beaming with big, dumb grins. I could practically hear the laughter coming from their jet as I just shook my head.

My hands were full flying the jet, and even if I had remembered my coin, I wouldn't have had sufficient skill at this point to extract it from my pocket while trying to not hit the other aircraft. I paid dearly that night for not honoring this tradition and bought several rounds of drinks for the others who did.

## Origins of the Challenge

Truth can be an elusive mistress. It would seem as if history itself can be changed with the flick of a pen or the stroke of a key. When it comes to stories — especially flying stories — the truth seems to be the enemy of entertainment. For this reason, the *10% Rule* was established early in the fighter pilot bar. I can attest to the fact that this law has been max-performed many times on a Friday night in the bar. I wish today that I could find the 100% truth to share with you regarding the history of the Challenge Coin, but alas, that truth has been through so many iterations of storytelling that I'm afraid it is gone forever. The military challenge coin is steeped in tradition, but its history is distorted and convoluted.

Without all the facts, and with several conflicting histories floating about in cyberspace, I will tell you the story of the Challenge Coin as it was described to me when I was a young, newly-winged 2nd Lieutenant in the U.S. Air Force. The story is based on the "facts" that were passed down through the oral tradition, but as with any story, it needs a little extra detail. The following is the history of how the Challenge Coin came to be.

## The "True" Legend of the Challenge Coin

A young American company-grade officer, whose name has long been forgotten, found himself alone at the controls of a British Sopwith Camel as the sun set over a raging ground battle in late summer, circa 1917. As with many of the pilots who had volunteered, our young 1st Lieutenant didn't have much flying experience and quickly found himself disoriented as visual conditions deteriorated with the waning light and the increasing smoke over the battlefield.

He had arrived in-theater only a week earlier, a recent graduate of Yale University looking for excitement and the opportunity to serve in uniform. Upon his arrival, he was relieved to see the familiar face of a fraternity brother of his from Yale leading one of the flights in the squadron.

Before departing on this particular mission, our protagonist's friend and flight commander presented him with a bronze medallion; a token of his induction into the squadron. Our lieutenant promptly put the medallion in a small leather pouch, which he hung around his neck before preparing his aircraft for flight. His heart raced as the wheels left the ground, and rightly so — he hadn't experienced the thrill of flight more than a handful of times, yet now he was being thrust into the throes of combat.

Upon reaching contested airspace, he was quickly separated from his flight mates. Wide-eyed, he strained his neck as he aggressively searched for his fellow airmen and any enemy aircraft that might be rolling in to fire upon him. As his eyes searched the heavens, it was only a matter of time before this young man's aircraft fell victim to ground artillery; something from which he thought he was immune as he circled the skies above the bloody fields below.

Desperately, he tried to maintain control. He looked for an open field towards which he could maneuver his crippled Sopwith. A grassy meadow just beyond a hedge practically called out to him as he descended, against his will, into enemy territory.

His wheels touched down hard, sinking into the soft ground causing his aircraft to flip over on its back, slamming the young pilot violently to the earth. As he regained consciousness, he found the muzzle of a German Mauser staring him in the face. He had been captured.

I'm not entirely sure what events took place over the next several days, but we go now to our young captive about a week after the crash—his body still bruised and aching from the impact. The Germans had taken everything from him, except the leather pouch, which was hung around his neck. He sat crouched in a makeshift cell somewhere near the battlefront; the burlap prisoner's garb kept any semblance of comfort from him.

Suddenly, the entire building shook violently as explosions rocked the compound. The young man's heart lifted. Surely, the Allies were assaulting the prison camp to rescue him! Several bomb-bursts eventually brought part of his building down, creating a gap in the exterior wall through which he quickly climbed. He emerged from the dilapidated building to find a scene of pure chaos. The bodies of German soldiers were strewn across the prison camp. The fence at the west end of the camp was down, and he ran toward it. He breached the fence but didn't stop running. His adrenaline carried him as he ran for his life.

Hours later, our hero found himself weak from hunger and exertion. He couldn't remember when he last ate, and his throat was parched from lack of water. He stumbled into a small farming settlement in search of sustenance. The French farmer who owned the farmstead met him with the barrel of a rifle. Our intrepid lieutenant thrust his arms skyward pleading in English, the only language he knew, for food and water. The French farmer was unfamiliar with the young man's American accent and took him to be a German.

The young officer was bound, thrown into the back of a wagon, and taken through the dark French countryside. When horse and wagon stopped, the lieutenant was met by a mob of angry Frenchmen. You see, there were several German scouts in the area masquerading as British soldiers. When the farmer didn't recognize the young man's accent, he decided to take him to a gathering of freedom fighters to find out what to do. This angry mob decided execution was the best course of action.

As they tied our shaken hero to the firing post, one of the Frenchmen saw the leather bag beneath his shirt. The bag was ripped from his neck and opened on the spot. The young man's captor took the medallion from the bag and held it up in the torchlight. After a few seconds of scrutiny, the Frenchman's eyes lit up, and the young man was released! The freedom fighter had recognized the squadron insignia emblazoned on the coin and knew right away the young man was no German. The medallion had saved the lieutenant's life! Our hero was given a bottle of the finest wine they had on hand and was soon returned to his squadron. Since that day, pilots have always carried a coin for good luck, and thus the Challenge Coin was born.

## Today's Challenge Coin Tradition (varies by military service—this is the Air Force's)

The tradition can best be explained by laying down the ground rules:

1. First of all, it's not called a "coin" unless you are invoking a challenge (except for purposes of describing the tradition or imparting these rules.) To avoid erroneously invoking a challenge, the item in question will be referred to as a Round Metal Object or RMO when not throwing down a challenge.

2. Ignorance can be claimed, but not by you! If you are the first to give someone a coin, you must explain the rules to him or her. If you fail to do so, you must pay up if that person unknowingly breaks the rules.

3. You must carry the coin with you at ALL times and in all places.

4. When challenged for your coin, you must produce it without taking more *than x* number of steps round-trip to retrieve it (the number of steps allowed varies by squadron—e.g. the 7th FS would allow you to take seven steps, the 27th FS would allow you to take 2.7 steps, etc.)

5. Failure to produce an RMO when challenged requires the purchase of a round of drinks for all those who have produced their coins. If multiple people fail to produce, multiple rounds are purchased.

6. If everyone who is challenged can produce their coin according to the above guidelines, then the challenger buys a drink for everyone challenged.

7. This tradition adheres to the concept of *every man/woman for himself/herself*. In other words, there is no helping or lending a coin to someone who has forgotten theirs.

8. Individual squadrons may invoke additional rules to the challenge coin tradition—as long as those rules are more restrictive in nature. An individual squadron's rules apply only to members of that squadron and will be scoffed heavily if erroneously applied to members of a different squadron.

9. Don't lose your RMO. If you lose your coin, you must find a suitable replacement. Your coin must never fall into the wrong hands. What are considered the wrong hands? Anyone's but yours.

10. The rules of this tradition apply to everyone who has been coined and continue to apply until death and maybe beyond. There's no way to tell for sure.

# Apologies

Apologies are typically not part of a fighter pilot's routine. This *Apologies* section is briefed only as a contingency! Maybe you accidentally discharged a fire extinguisher in the dorms of Squadron Officer School while defending your honor in a harmless game of chicken. (It's been done before.) Or perhaps you stole your sister squadron's mascot and in the process accidentally shattered the window of their squadron commander's office... again. Or let's just say you walked into the Wing Administration building and let loose on some ground-pounder who works three hours before lunch and spends the rest of the day at squadron PT — he calls it "training" — instead of helping you during the only hour of the day you are free.

Whatever the reason may be, you will likely be required by someone higher ranking than you to apologize to someone far inferior to you. (The word *apologize* invokes a slight vomiting response in the throat of the fighter pilot. I'm having a difficult time writing this.)

Fear not! The lieutenants of fighter squadrons around the world have it all figured out. Just fill out the form below and submit it to the offended party. Boom. You're all set. Just make sure it's on official letterhead.

MEMORANDUM FOR WHOM IT MAY CONCERN

FROM: Squadron Apology Officer

SUBJECT: We're Sorry!

1. The Fighter Pilots of (insert your squadron here) apologize for the following reason(s):

- Golfing while intoxicated / rolling the golf cart
- Walking while intoxicated
- Singing while intoxicated
- Singing "I Love My Wife" in your squadron
- Stealing stuff from your squadron
- Missed appointment at the Dental Hobby Shop
- Calling your dental clinic a "Hobby Shop"
- Breaking your windows
- Not wearing a hat from our car to the O'Club
- Taking over your squadron/private bar for an impromptu Roll Call
- Pissing off (circle one) Security Forces / your wife / the locals / random people, for doing _____ again
- Breaking bottles on your fancy beach

- Drag racing the rental minivans with the gun doors open
- Ransacking random houses looking for car keys
- Late OPR/EPR/Award/Decoration
- Puking in (circle one) _____'s office / on the fridge / in your lunch
- Whatever it is we don't remember
- Beating the crap out of you for not doing your job
- Blanket apology (to be marked only when apologizing for actions in advance for the next six months.)

//Signed//

Name Here

Apology Officer, (Your Squadron Here)

# The Joy and Pain of TDY

Seville, Spain is nice in the fall. The city is alive with bustling traffic, leisurely tourists, and persistent street vendors. But when the sun goes down, the city goes to sleep early. One evening, I found myself wandering the *calles* with my fellow Black Sheep long after the sun had set. The activity of the day had abruptly ceased as shops and restaurants closed. The city was all but fast asleep by 10 p.m.

We continued to weave our way in and out of the city streets until we found a food and beverage establishment, an Irish pub, that was still open. As one of the few places in the city still doing business, it attracted a lot of night owls. It wasn't long before a group of exchange students from the U.S., Great Britain, and France had attached themselves firmly to our group. What can I say? They wanted to be in the presence of greatness. Can you blame them?

The night wore on, and we eventually tired of the pub and the crowd. Seeking to experience more of the city, we left the bar with the group of students in trail. They were enamored with the concept of partying with fighter pilots and didn't seem to mind being ignored.

The students had said they knew of another bar that was open several blocks away, so we set a course for the new destination. On our way, one of the Instructor Pilots in my squadron, Bandit, began to let the drink get the best of him. Bandit, who had the skinny frame of a long-distance runner, began randomly challenging members of our group to a dual. Against my better judgement, I asked him what he meant.

Within minutes, Bandit and I were engaged on a full-on wrestling match there in the streets of Seville. The poor exchange students were terrified. The ugly Americans had become violent and one of the French girls began to cry.

"It's ok," I yelled as I started choking Bandit out. "We're friends!"

It wasn't long before the large following we had attracted was completely dispersed and both Bandit and I were covered in dirt and blood. Five minutes later, we had our arms around each other's shoulder smiling at the bouncer in front of a Spanish night club. He judged our disheveled appearance, and wasn't about to give us entrance to his establishment. I couldn't blame him.

Fighter pilots get sick of flying around the proverbial flag pole all the time (*flying around the flag pole* means staying in the local airspace.) Every opportunity to leave *home station* must be taken to increase morale and enhance training. Temporary Duty (TDY) is an important part of the fighter pilot's lifestyle. TDY is where legends are born, and reputations are made.

It is not entirely out of the question for one to go TDY as a single person and come home married. It is also not outside the realm of possibilities for one to depart on a quick TDY financially stable and come home bankrupt (TDYs to Vegas can be especially brutal.) If you can dream it, it's probably happened while on TDY.

Without a baseline understanding of the type of behavior that is appropriate for a fighter pilot while TDY, the various personalities in a squadron would run amok causing a complete collapse of the delicate social ecosystem that we work so hard to maintain. For the squadron to survive a TDY, everyone must be on the same page and adhere to a certain set of rules. The rules are in place for the well-being of the group. So, if you're the new guy or gal in a fighter squadron, learn your squadron's TDY Rules. Here are a few to get you started.

## Rules of TDY

1. *Don't be a limfac.* Limfac is short for *limiting factor.* There are several ways to be a limfac, and many are addressed in these rules. If you aren't a limfac by nature, you'll have no problem following the rest of the rules.

2. *Don't smile while you pack.* Your significant other must truly believe you are so sad to leave her/him as you take off on your three-week TDY to Las Vegas. It's a hard job to keep the casinos in business, but someone's got to do it!

3. *Always bring cash.* Don't be the guy searching for an ATM when everyone else is making it rain.

4. *No cameras shall be used to document your TDY!* A picture is worth a thousand words, but sometimes ten thousand words are required to explain what you are doing walking down the Vegas Strip in your underwear with a flame-thrower in your hands and a football helmet on your noggin. These aren't the Kodak moments you want to share.

5. *Don't miss the push.* In combat, the push time is sacred. It is the time when the forces are rallied and begin to push their way into bad guy land to strike a target. You may not all come home at the same time, but you all push together on time. The same goes for the push on TDY. Taxis can be expensive. Was it truly worth missing the push to get that extra 10 minutes of sleep?

6. *Don't be tired.* There are plenty of energy options available for you to keep pace with the rest of the squadron. The reality is that everyone is as tired as you, but we all fake it so we don't end up spending every night of the TDY in the hooch (the dorms/lodging.)

7. *Embrace the Combat Split.* When the dinner bill arrives, it is too time-consuming to separate the tickets. Fighter pilots on TDY have places to go and things to burn! The check will be split equally amongst all who partook (the exception to this rule is rule #12.) Be sure to have some awareness as to what is going on at the table around you. If everyone is going big, it's time to spring for that Market Priced Lobster. I knew one particularly unlucky fellow who showed up late to a dinner, ordered a water and clam chowder and walked away with an $80 bill. Be sure to get your money's worth!

8. *Drive it like a rental... because it is.* Fighter pilots must max-perform every piece of machinery with which they come in contact. This rule doesn't require you to destroy your rental vehicle! (You wouldn't intentionally crash your jet, right?) That said, rental car tires are expected to be returned bald.

9. *No spouses or significant others are allowed on the TDY.* If one spouse comes along, the others may feel jealous or upset they weren't invited. It's best just to avoid this potential can of worms.

10. *Never fly with the rental car keys in your pocket.* This is a cardinal sin. How can the bros make a lunch push to the Thai restaurant du jour if the keys to your only rental vehicle are pulling 9 Gs at 20,000 feet? Empty stomachs and baseball bats will meet

you as you step triumphantly from your aircraft upon landing if you take the keys flying.

11. *Never abandon a bro downtown.* The wingman concept applies just as much in downtown Las Vegas as it does in an ACM engagement. Mutual support is imperative if everyone is to make it safely back to the hooch at the end of the night.

12. *The driver never pays for dinner.* If you're going to drink your face off and are fortunate enough to have a bro be your personal chauffeur for the evening, you *will* take care of him.

13. *Always pay your landing fee* — but only after complaining to the Snack-O that the fee is ridiculously high. The Snack Officer (Snack-O) must keep the coffers of the morale fund overflowing but cannot do so with your money. The fee you are charged upon arrival at your TDY location (the landing fee) is used to make life better for you and the other pilots in your unit. But let's face it, you were abused when you were the Snack-O, now it's your turn to give out the good-natured punishment. Besides, you wouldn't have to pay the $200 landing fee for two weeks on the road if the LPA knew how to manage the squadron money. However, just like the bros paid their landing fees when you were the Snack-O, you *will* pay yours. You're making extra money on TDY, and it needs to go to the poor lieutenants who typically bankroll the Snack-O fund.

14. *A health night is permitted for TDYs greater than one week in length.* We can all rage for a week, but even the best jet engines in the world cannot sustain operations in afterburner indefinitely. Health nights may be taken under the following circumstances: a) You have raged for a solid week and internal organs threaten to leave you if you push it up one more night. b) You did something stupid like blow all your cash for the TDY on the first night—this is more considered a punishment night than a health night. c) You are the mission commander for the next day's LFE and you brief before 5:00 a.m. If you are a wingman, you are expected to rage with the rest of the bros, because you probably haven't done anything to help your flight lead in mission planning anyway, so why start now?

15. *No live-Tweeting, -Facebook-ing, etc. of your TDY.* This mainly applies to the SNAPs (Sensitive New Age Pilots) who can't seem to disconnect from the online world. Such SNAP behavior falls into the category of poor OPSEC (Operational Security), and nothing could spoil a TDY more than someone finding out you're not home and taking advantage of that knowledge to relieve you of your possessions.

16. *Never come home tired.* Mama has been missing you, and you need to come home energized, or she may not let you leave again! Your significant other's happiness is paramount to continued TDY

success. Do whatever it takes to make mama happy.

## Not All Fun and Games

A flying squadron must go on the road for improved training opportunities. While the aforementioned rules may seem whimsical and fun, they truly serve a purpose: to maintain conformity, unity, and safety of the group. A cohesive group of fighter pilots will be more likely to receive effective training. If someone is not accepted by the group socially, it will be more difficult, though not impossible, for them to gain trust in the tactical realm.

TDYs typically require a higher workload than operations at home. The days are longer and meals can sometimes be few and far between based on time constraints. The good news is, queep (nonflying-related duty) is mostly left at home allowing the fighter pilot to focus primarily on tactics. An emphasis on tactics is the main reason TDYs are not only good but necessary for a modern fighter squadron. Fighter pilot TDY traditions lend to the overall effectiveness of the unit and heightened morale.

# The Four-Letter F-Word

I stood before the gathering of fighter pilots with my cranium hung low. The room was mostly silent as I forced the bitter words from my mouth.

"My name is Rob, and I'm a frat-er."

The room erupted in a series of boos and hisses as people threw popcorn, empty beer cans, and even a pizza box at me. They had every right to do so. The only thing helping me keep it together was the amazing lesson I had learned in the process of committing the four-letter F-word. So how did I end up in such a brutal and embarrassing situation? What four-letter F-word am I talking about? This chapter isn't easy to write (and it may be a difficult one to read); nevertheless, it's important to understand how seriously a fighter pilot approaches fratricide and what we do to ensure it never happens in real life.

The dreaded four-letter F-word (*frat*, short for fratricide — the accidental killing of one friendly troop by another) happened while I was a student completing a course called Introduction to Fighter Fundamentals (IFF). During IFF, the fledgling fighter pilot learns the basics — and I mean the *basics* — of dogfighting and Air Combat Maneuvering (ACM). I had recently completed the Basic Fighter Maneuvers (BFM) portion of the course and was working my way through the last ACM rides.

In ACM, the student fighter pilot flies as the wingman in a two-ship formation and works with the flight lead to kill a bandit (enemy aircraft) as quickly and efficiently as possible. There is a lot of radio communication involved as flight lead and wingman work together to ensure the bandit is properly identified and that weapons are employed against him. The "gotcha" of ACM happens when like-kind aircraft are training against each other, and the shooter misidentifies a friendly aircraft as the hostile bandit.

Such was the case for me one fine December afternoon in the skies over San Antonio, Texas. My flight lead and I took off from Randolph AFB and climbed through the clouds to our fight airspace. Our bandit for the day, a highly experienced IFF Instructor, took off shortly after us and orchestrated a rejoin once we were all established above the clouds in our working area.

After accomplishing our Fence Checks and a G-awareness exercise (two high-G turns of 180 degrees), my flight lead made the radio call to get everyone ready for the fight.

"Next setup will be ACM for Saber Flight. Saber One is ready," he said, his voice crackling over the radio.

"Saber Two is ready!" I acknowledged.

"Bandit's ready!" replied our resident bad guy.

"Bandit, Saber, cleared to maneuver," said my flight lead as the fight commenced.

I was in tactical formation, one mile directly off the right side of my flight lead's aircraft. I strained my neck to the left as I searched the six o'clock position of my flight lead, trying to locate the bandit. As I was searching, I received a frantic radio call from my flight lead.

"Saber Two, break right, flare. Bandit your six o'clock, two miles!"

The bandit had decided to pick on me for this fight. I obeyed my flight lead's directive without hesitation. My left hand pushed both throttles all the way forward to select full afterburner while my right hand yanked the control stick to the right rolling my jet sharply to commence a break turn into the bandit. This maximum performance turn in the direction of my adversary would deny his ability to fire a short-range missile at me. I swung around in my seat to look back as far as I could behind my aircraft trying to gain a tally (visual contact) on the bandit. As I looked to my deep six, another excited radio call burst through my headset.

"Saber Two, bandit switched! Saber One's engaged!" said my flight lead.

"Saber Two!" I replied as I struggled to find the bandit who was now a little over one mile behind me.

The bandit had ceased his attack on me, picked up a tally on my flight lead, and switched his attack to Saber One. In doing so, the bandit had initiated a turn away from me, making it harder for me to spot him.

I flexed the muscles in my quadriceps as the sustained 6G turn was beginning to make my blood pool in my legs, potentially leading to G-induced loss of consciousness. The flexing and breathing techniques taught to me in pilot training helped keep the blood in my brain while preserving my eyesight. *Grey out* is a common reason fighter pilots lose sight of a bandit in an engagement. One of the axioms of BFM is "lose sight, lose fight." I needed to see the bandit ASAP if I wanted my two-ship to survive this engagement.

After a few more seconds of turn, I spotted both aircraft. Two T-38Cs, with the same paint scheme, now tumbled and turned in the sky before me. It was a beautiful, but deadly ballet that was playing out as they had entered a one-circle fight in the vertical. After a brief pause to enjoy the small victory of visually sighting the sparring aircraft, I knew I had to figure out who was who.

"Saber Two is tally two. Status, high/low," I said, doing my best to sound calm while letting my flight lead know I had two aircraft in sight. My heart was pounding, both from the recently completed high-G break turn and from the massive amount of adrenaline coursing through my veins. With my radio call, I had asked my flight lead if he was the high aircraft in the fight, or if he was below the bandit. In the T-38C, descriptive communication was the only way to identify a friend from a foe.

"Saber One is the high man, high man!" said my flight lead.

"Saber One, press!" I said, indicating I knew who was who in the zoo and that I was going to assume the supporting role.

Unbeknownst to me at the time, my flight lead's perspective of the horizon was impaired by the layers of clouds below and around the airspace. In the tumbling vertical fight, he had perceived that he was the high man when it would have appeared to me that he was the low man, causing me to identify him as the bandit.

After his next merge with the bandit, I waited until I had a clean shot, then I pressed the pickle button, releasing a simulated Aim-9 into the aircraft I thought was the bad guy.

"Fox 2," I called out on the radio. "Kill bandit, low man in a left-hand turn at 12,000."

"Bandit copies kill," replied our adversary as we ceased tactical maneuvering and commenced the knock-it-off drill.

I felt like King Kong as we walked back into the squadron after the sortie. The feeling of excitement wouldn't last long before turning to one of absolute disgust in the tape review. As we put the puzzle pieces of the mission together, we saw that the "low man" I had killed on that first setup was my flight lead. My stomach turned as my mind came to grips with the fact that I had shot a missile, albeit a simulated one, at a friendly aircraft.

## The Fog and Friction of War

As perplexing as my training scenario was to me that day early in my career, real combat situations are much more complex and confusing. Hostile airspace can have a host of aircraft flying around in it, and the fighter pilot must distinguish not only the identity of each but also whether or not each aircraft has met the Rules of Engagement (ROE) qualifying it to be fired upon.

While friendly players are typically participants in a datalink that helps pilots and Air Battle Managers keep track of the good guys, the datalink doesn't always work. Aircraft discrepancies can make identifying a friendly aircraft difficult, if not impossible at times. Add to the mix all the deceptive radar jamming and possible surface-to-air employment on the part of the enemy, and you have a recipe for disaster. If the fighter pilot is not knowledgeable and disciplined enough to adhere to the ROE, bad things can happen.

The onus is on the fighter pilot to know who is being targeted before pressing the Weapons Release Switch. Friendly lives have been lost as a result of undisciplined weapons employment.

## The Tradition

The evening after I committed the dreaded four-letter F-word, I found myself dressed in my flight suit on the doorstep of my flight lead's home. I took a deep breath as my right hand went for the doorbell; my left hand occupied with a bouquet of flowers for the "dead" pilot's wife. In the fighter squadron, we consider ourselves to be family, and when one family member unwittingly employs ordnance on another, simulated or otherwise, we make sure we do the right thing to help their family get through the tragedy.

My flight lead's wife laughed about the experience. It was just another silly fighter pilot tradition to her, but I felt otherwise. What if the scenario had been real combat, and the simulated missile a live Aim-9? How would I feel seeing my bro's jet burst into a fireball before me? How would I feel ringing this doorbell to face the wife of the man who died at my hands because I made an incorrect assessment?

The tradition of taking flowers to the spouse of a pilot you "frat-ed" is an important one. It causes everyone in the squadron, not just the pilot who pressed the pickle button, to stop and put things into perspective. Facing the family members of those you fly with makes you take your job more seriously and helps you realize how important it is to be the very best you can be.

That week's Roll Call found me in front of the bros confessing — the same way a member of Alcoholics Anonymous would confess — my dastardly deed earlier in the week. I had paid penance to the family of the pilot I shot down, now it was time to pay penance to the bros. Anyone who commits fratricide in a training scenario is required to buy the next keg of beer for the squadron bar. I had forked over the money earlier in the day to fill the mugs of those present at Roll Call.

After the requisite razzing of having popcorn, Solo cups, and pizza boxes thrown at me, the room quieted down as I described the heart-wrenching scenario. As I spoke, other pilots in the rooms swore to themselves they would never make the same mistake. That's the point of publicly shaming someone who commits fratricide. Hopefully, someone would learn from my mistake.

## Flip-Side of the Coin

Five years later, I found myself as the flight lead of a four-ship of F-22s in a large combat exercise. The fog and friction of the simulated combat scenario were thick. I had just cleared a merge and was flowing to protect a strike package consisting of F-15Es when I was told I had been killed and to kill-remove back to the Blue Air Safe Zone. My wingman, who was supporting me to my merge, had unwittingly shot me as I previously engaged in BFM with a bandit.

That night, as my bro showed up to my house with flowers in hand for my wife, I reflected on my experience in IFF. My commander at the time told me, "Son, there are those who have frat-ed and those who will. You are now one who has. Don't let it happen again." The lesson I learned five years earlier was a lesson my wingman learned this day. Hopefully, his lesson would serve him as well as mine had served me.

Fighter pilot traditions, such as those invoked when a fratricide incident takes place, can help a young pilot learn a lesson that will never be forgotten. It is better to learn through injured pride on a training sortie than through the spilling of friendly blood in combat. It is, for this reason, our traditions must never die!

# Piano Burning

Pianos don't come cheap these days. Why on earth would someone burn a perfectly good one? Fighter pilots burn a lot of things, so what's special about an ivory-keyed music apparatus? As with many of our traditions, this mysterious ritual has its origins in the British Royal Air Force (RAF). And, as always, if it began in England, chances are it makes for a magnificent story. We're going to explore the colorful history of this cerebral ceremony and illustrate the depth of the mark it can make on the life of a fighter pilot.

## Origins of Arson

The first men to take to the skies with the intent to kill were not what you'd probably expect them to be. They weren't bloodthirsty soldiers who had merely found a new method for their macabre work. No, these men were gentlemen of the highest order! Early British fighter pilots were members of high society. They were well-educated, cultured men — and they were a precious few.

But these polished men didn't last long in the early wars of attrition. A great number of them died during the first World War.

As the lives of these refined fighter pilots were claimed through the exploratory days of military combat aviation, the pool of gentlemen pilots dwindled. There arose a need to recruit the successors of these early aristocrats from the heaving masses of the *commoners.* Although the blood lineage of fighter pilots changed, the high standard to which they were held did not.

The fighter pilot was expected to be a well-mannered man who could impress a lady with the way he waltzed. He was supposed to recite poetry and understand the most intricate facets of science and art. He was expected to continue in the die cast by his predecessors.

Part of this heritage involved an expectation that combat pilots should play the piano. Many of the new aviation recruits at the time felt more comfortable bellying up to the bar than reciting Shakespeare, much less playing such a complicated instrument. Nevertheless, piano lessons were a requisite and were taught in officers' clubs across England. As you can imagine, the new breed of fighter pilot did not take kindly to being forced to perform such a mundane task.

The image of the fighter pilot was forever changed by events set in motion by a freak accident at an RAF air base. The O'Club had burned down at RAF Leuchars and with it, the only piano on base. Piano lessons were canceled indefinitely. Word of the cancellations spread, and a light turned on in the minds of fighter pilots everywhere. The answer to the piano lesson problem was so simple! Burn the musical monsters and end the lessons! And so it was that pianos throughout the RAF were dragged outside and burned in defiance of the ridiculous requirement. From that moment on, the fighter pilot was forever redefined.

## When to Burn

If you happen to find yourself at the club on a Friday night, chances are you won't see flames reaching high into the heavens or smell the burning rosewood and melting copper. No, piano burnings are not something that takes place regularly (due in part to previously mentioned financial constraints.) Fighter pilots only pull out the lighters and gasoline with the intent to burn on very special occasions. There is no set list of such moments, and the basic criteria for determining if the situation merits a burned piano is simple: there must be a piano available and the bar must be stocked.

Pianos ripe for burning seem to magically appear coincident with events such as a squadron deactivation, the graduation of a pilot training class, the passing of a fellow fighter pilot, etc. When the need to burn a piano arises, one will appear.

## An Indelible Mark

It had been a fantastic year for the 8th Fighter Squadron. In addition to my indoctrination into the fighter pilot community, my first year in an actual fighter squadron was wrought with several TDYs, a squadron reunion, and a deployment to the Middle East. Mustaches were grown, bank accounts were wiped clean, reprimands from commanding officers were endured, and we had all survived with minimal scarring. I was thrilled to have experienced a wide array of adventures with such a great group of aviators.

So, it was with much sadness that I went about helping to plan the deactivation ceremony for the Black Sheep. Yes, the BRAC (Base Realignment and Closure) list had another kill to paint on its theoretical fuselage: the 8th Fighter Squadron.

The Black Sheep had been reactivated following a brief period of inactivity between the decommissioning of the F-117 Nighthawk and the arrival of the F-22 at Holloman Air Force Base, New Mexico. The reactivation ceremony, held just one year before, was full of excitement and hope as we looked to a bright future flying Raptors with 8 FS tail flashes. Now, we all bemoaned its closing and began coming to terms with the fact that the band was about to break up.

We had to honor the Black Sheep heritage one more time before putting the unit to rest—possibly for the last time as a fighter squadron. We had to do something truly monumental to leave a deep impression in everyone's mind, reminding them of the squadron mantra, "Once a Sheep... ALWAYS A SHEEP!" We had to plan an epic party.

The day of the deactivation ceremony arrived. The afternoon consisted of a flyover and some pomp and circumstance associated with the ceremonial passing of the guidon. The Public Affairs office was out in force, relentlessly snapping photos to document the occasion. They hoped to preserve the moment for future generations of Black Sheep if the squadron were ever to be resurrected.

As night fell, most of the base leadership and administrative personnel departed. Once our dreary quorum was left alone, every Black Sheep pilot, along with the pilots of our sister squadron, found his way to the squadron bar. At precisely 8:08 p.m., the door to the crowded bar slammed shut like a clap of thunder, as Mac—our honorable Mayor—yelled, "Haaaaaaaaaaack!" commencing Roll Call for the last time in the Black Sheep bar. A thick cloud of cigar smoke hung in the air as all talking ceased.

The Roll Call was bittersweet. We followed the same agenda we did for all the other Roll Calls. As the night wore on, the laughter and enjoyment continued. Just before midnight, after the last story was imparted, and the last joke told, Mac solemnly ordered the singing of the Whiffenpoof Song, possibly for the last time in a fighter squadron bar. The haunting melody moved everyone in the room. Had fighter pilots been cursed with tear ducts, there would not have been a dry eye in the room.

With that, the Roll Call was closed. Under the direction of our Mayor, and with the assistance of several sober cat-herders like myself, the inebriated masses migrated out back behind the squadron for the culminating moment of the evening's events: the piano burning.

A majestic upright had magically appeared in the center of a large cement pad, complete with a couple of gallons of gasoline. A crew of pyromaniac squadron mates doused the piano in the flammable liquid. With a nod from the Mayor, a torchbearer appeared and touched the embers of the burning stick to the gasoline-soaked piano. We all watched solemnly as the flames leaped up into the starry canopy above us. For several minutes, the only sound was the crackling of the blaze before us. Someone started singing. I don't recall what song it was, but one by one we all joined in. The piano burned brightly as we sang song after song.

Gradually, the solemnness gave way once again to the jovial spirit that prevailed earlier in the night. When the once intact wooden instrument had burned down to a molten lump no higher than about three feet, the feats of strength began. People tried jumping over the fire. Some even tried throwing other people into it. That night, in front of a burning piano, we were fighter pilots. Sure, we weren't in our cockpits slinging missiles in defense of freedom. But we were connecting with fighter pilots past. We were strengthening the bonds of brotherhood that would carry us one day into combat, and bring us home—all of us—together.

Years later, I would reflect briefly on this night from my cockpit over hostile territory. The bright orange lights below me, byproducts of a firestorm of precision guided munitions, reminded me of that distant night behind the 8th Fighter Squadron. Hearing the voices of my flight mates — my bros — on the radio reminded me of the camaraderie solidified by the embers of the burning piano. We were trusting our lives to each other, and we would die to protect each other if it came to it. Funny how a little thing like a burning piano stays with you.

# The Tactical Debrief

Fighter pilots must have thick skins. Nowhere is this more important than in the tactical debrief. It is critical that each pilot involved in a combat training mission learn from his or her mistakes. There is not enough time to pull punches and avoid hurting people's feelings. Time must be used efficiently, and everyone involved must not take criticism personally. The debrief makes the fighter pilot better.

There's a lot to cover in a big Air Combat Training mission. The debrief usually kicks off with a shot evaluation/validation that takes about an hour. The air-to-air and air-to-ground shot evaluations (known simply as *the Shot Eval*) is simply a playback of the mission from a God's-Eye view on a big screen. The playback is stopped when weapons are employed to review release and termination parameters. After the Shot Eval, the adversaries are cleared off, and Blue Air meets to go over the lessons learned from the sortie. The Blue Air debrief is spent reviewing the tapes (audio and video recordings from the individual aircraft), listening to the recorded radio calls, and analyzing game plans and execution. All of this is done to make sure the mistakes made on that training mission aren't made again. It can be a very long process.

### Debrief Etiquette

As with everything in the fighter pilot's life, there is a right way and a wrong way to do things. In general, the debrief is standardized to efficiently convey lessons learned from the sortie. Deviations from the standard typically end in mutinous disaster.

Here are a few basic rules for surviving the debrief:

1. The mission commander/flight lead conducting the debrief must stand. Standing establishes dominance, but may not maintain it. Read on.
2. Wingmen do not interrupt the debriefer. The only exception to this rule is if your bladder is about to explode because you didn't plan appropriately before the briefing room door closed. Just fess up, take your lashings, and get it over with!
3. Use chalk to debrief BFM, markers to debrief ACT.
4. Eat or drink during the debrief only after receiving permission from the person conducting the debrief.

5. Do whatever it takes to stay awake. Do you still have a Go Pill left over from that last ocean crossing? You may want to save it for Roll Call, but don't hesitate to break it out if your flight lead starts to sound like the teacher from the movie *Ferris Beuller's Day Off.*

6. Never interrupt someone else's debrief. It doesn't matter if the building is on fire. Have faith that the briefing room will be the last to burn as it is protected by the awesomeness of the learning taking place inside.

Each flight lead has a different style of debriefing. Some have been known to get angry and hurl chairs, chalk, and other inanimate objects across the room. Others are known for droning on, quietly putting their audience to sleep before finally arriving at their point. The best debriefers can succinctly identify lessons from the mission and cover them in such a way as to make an impression on their audience. If the debrief is dragging on, you might hear someone in the room say, "Faster and funnier!"

## Red Flag Debrief

Exercise Red Flag is one of the biggest Large Force Exercises in the United States Military. All branches of the military participate, as do many of our NATO and coalition partners. During the two- to three-week-long exercise, hundreds of aircraft may be airborne at any given time. With so many moving parts and pieces, it takes a significant amount of time to extract lessons learned from the engagements and debrief them appropriately.

I was a newly minted F-22 wingman when I first attended a Red Flag. Our Squadron Weapons Officer, a mid-level Captain, had just led our eight-ship through a very complex, hard-fought mission and several mistakes were made. We had landed just after four o'clock p.m. and had spent the past six hours reviewing our tapes, getting weapons release parameters, and debriefing with our adversaries.

By the time each participating squadron had split off to debrief on their own, we had been in the building for over eight hours. At this point, we noticed many of the other squadrons calling it a day—all of them, in fact. My squadron was the only one in the vault still briefing. Our Weapons Officer starting cueing up our tapes one by one to review them when our Ops Group Commander, a crusty old Colonel who had flown as a wingman in the mission, spoke up.

"Son, are we going to watch every minute of the two-hour mission eight times? I think we're done in this setting. We can debrief the rest at Blueberry Hill."

The Weapons Officer's mouth dropped open. How dare a wingman speak to his flight lead like this?! But seeing as the vocal wingman was the Ops Group Commander, the Patch made the tactical decision to follow orders.

"Blueberry Hill sounds good, sir," said the Weapons Officer through clenched teeth.

The rest of us quietly rejoiced as we packed up the room and headed to our favorite open-all-night restaurant outside the Nellis Air Force Base main gate. It was then that I realized I hadn't had anything to eat for about eight hours.

The Ops Group Commander taught an important lesson that night. It doesn't matter how good the teacher is, the student must be willing and able to learn. Each fighter pilot has a *time of useful consciousness* during which lessons must be internalized before the thousand-yard stare sets in. For me that night, a stack of pancakes was just what I needed to recover from the hours of learning!

### Wrapping it Up

I believe the purpose of the debrief is the same as honoring tradition: to make pilots better. The fighter pilots of yesterday have set a strong, solid example. The pilots of today would be fools to depart from such a high standard. Although we may do things differently in the squadron today, the intent behind our actions remains the same.

Tradition fills a fighter pilot with pride; it bonds us together. Tradition makes us better pilots and better people. Isn't that who you want up there in the skies keeping watch over you and your family? It is for these reasons tradition will forever remain a part of the fighter pilot culture.

# Fighter Pilot Speak

So far, I've dedicated each chapter of this book to a specific fighter pilot tradition. No compendium of fighter pilot traditions will ever truly be complete given the impossible nature of capturing every detail that is part of the fighter pilot culture. Separate books could be written for each tradition I have outlined, but there just isn't enough time in the day to dive into such detail, especially when there's flying yet to be done!

Fighter pilots speak their own language, both verbally and non-verbally. This chapter will serve as a glossary in helping you understanding our method of communication. It is an abbreviated list of acronyms and initials used in this book and some simple terms and gestures you may hear or see around a fighter squadron. It is not intended to be an exhaustive list of fighter pilot vocabulary. I don't think the People Obligated to Observe Political Correctness (POOPCor) — the pseudo-regulatory institution that seems to rule modern America — would allow it.

**"A"-word** - Derogatory term used to refer to an airliner. None of us will admit it, but we all believe we'll end up flying one someday.

**ACM** - Air Combat Engagement. Two or more "good guys" (typically a flight lead and a wingman) working together to kill multiple bandits.

**AMRAAM** - (Pronounced "Am-Ram") The affectionate name for the Aim-120, an Active Medium Range Air-to-Air Missile. The AMRAAM may also be referred to as the fighter pilot's "skinny wingman."

**B-Course** - The basic instructional course where pilots first learn to fly a specific type of fighter. It is also referred to as the "School House."

**Bandit** - An enemy aircraft that has been identified as a foe. This term can also be used to describe someone (e.g. a non-flying admin-type person) who refuses to do their job and support the fighter pilot.

**BFM** - Basic Fighter Maneuvers. This is just a formal way of referring to a dogfight. BFM is considered amongst fighter pilots to be the *Sport of Kings*. Reputations are made and lost on one's ability to fly BFM. We all think we're the best and that everyone else sucks at BFM… because it's true.

**Bingo** - A pre-briefed fuel state requiring immediate return to base (RTB.) It basically means you're out of gas and have to go home. When someone in your flight tells you they are "bingo", you clear them off so they don't flame out. It's also a nonchalant way to tell your bros you're out of cash when you're at the casino.

**Blue Air** - The good guys in the fight. Blue Air executes full-up tactics and does their best to destroy Red Air in the most efficient, merciless way possible. The term originated from early war games when the good guys would wear blue bands on their uniform to differentiate themselves from the bad guys in the training scenario.

**Bogey** - An aircraft of unknown allegiance. Also, used to refer to someone who is very temperamental. Is it a good guy? Is it a bad guy? I guess we'll see!

**BVR** - Beyond Visual Range. This term is used when engaging an enemy at range, typically with an AMRAAM. When a fighter pilot receives an e-mail (aka "gonk mail") with a task from a superior ranking officer, it is referred to as a *BVR tasking*.

**CAP** - Combat Air Patrol. A CAP is essentially a holding pattern where the fighter pilot waits, like a pitbull on a leash, to fling hate at his enemy.

**Chaff** - A defensive expenditure used to deny a firing solution by enemy radar. If it works to keep radar guided missiles on the rails of enemy jets, maybe it will keep you from getting tasked on the ground by your boss. If you know you're being targeted, chaff it off!

**CT** - Continuation Training. No grade sheet, no worries, just raging!

**CODE 1** - The jet has no discrepancies and can fly again without maintenance action.

**CODE 2** - The jet has minor discrepancies, but can still fly.

**CODE 3** - Dude, I broke the jet. Sorry, but this baby isn't getting airborne without some serious work.

**Crew Chief** - The maintainer in charge of ensuring your jet is prepped and ready to fly. These guys and gals spend endless hours in the hot sun, the rain, and the snow to make sure you get to go do the mission. If you take care of your crew chief, your crew chief will take care of you! On special occasions, if you're really lucky, they will perform a freestyle dance as you taxi out.

**Deceased Insect** - This is a little game played in a packed fighter pilot bar. If someone yells out "DEAD BUG!", everyone must drop to the floor, lie on their backs, and put their hands and feet in the air similar to the way a dead bug would. The last one to assume the position buys the bar. This game is slowly fading from the fighter pilot bar as the amount of broken glass, spilled beverages, and other uncomfortable items on the bar floor have increased. The origin of this game is unknown.

**Doofer Book** - This the written record of all the idiotic/funny/ridiculous things that happen in a fighter squadron and who perpetrates them. The book is kept by the Scribe and can be updated throughout the week as required so the week's asinine activities can be recounted at Roll Call. Don't worry; *everyone* ends up in the Doofer Book at some point—just try to minimize your exposure!

**Elbow Pointing** - Pointing with your finger is not polite, as the good people of South Korea will tell you. Fighter pilots who spent a significant amount of time there had to think of another visual signal to use in place of pointing. Why not pick something ridiculous like pointing with your elbow? The habit followed them back to the states and now we all do it.

**Fence Check** - Tactical checklist for ensuring appropriate system settings are squared away before crossing over the "fence" (enemy territory.) It is conducted while airborne and typically involves ensuring your weapons are properly armed or safed. You "fence in" on your way to your objective, and you "fence out" on your way home. The term may also be used when visiting an agency on base outside of the fighter squadron. Going to see the finance clerks about how they screwed up your pay? You better *fence in*.

**Flare** - Infrared countermeasure used in self-defense against a heat seeking missile. It is also used as a term to describe one's defensive actions when backpedaling after saying something stupid to one's spouse.

**Flight Lead** - The fighter pilot in charge of the formation. A flight (for tactical purposes) typically is made up of four aircraft. The flight can be subdivided into two elements of two. In a four-ship formation, the pilots flying in the number one and number three positions are flight leads. If you're not number one in the formation, your job is to back number one up.

**FLUG** - Flight Lead Upgrade. Every wingman's deepest desire — to become the person in charge!

**Fox 2** - Communication brevity indicating you've just fired a heat-seeking missile.

**Fox 3** - Communication brevity indicating you've just fired a radar-guided missile. By now you're wondering what happened to Fox 1? The term Fox 1 was phased out by most friendly forces with the passing of the Aim-7 Sparrow missile and is now typically reserved for use by Red Air.

**Frat** - A four-letter F-word and the worst sin a fighter pilot can commit. It is short for *fratricide* and happens when a friendly fighter mistakenly targets another friendly aircraft. See the chapter titled The Four-Letter F-Word.

**Gonk** - Fighter pilots are resistant to change when it comes to anything except tactics. When computers were first introduced as a means of doing paperwork in the fighter squadron, they were derogatorily referred to as *gonks*. The moniker stuck for a couple of decades but is slowly phasing out as the Shoe Clerks (see definition below) continue to find other ways to annoy fighter pilots.

**Gonk Mail** - Derogatory term for email. Nothing good comes to a fighter pilot via email.

**Go Pills** - When you're the only pilot on board the aircraft, and you have to fly for eight hours or more, the flight doc will typically issue you a powerful no-doze pill (Dextroamphetamine is normally issued.) This helps to ensure you don't fall asleep when the LPA fails to provide in-flight entertainment on a long ocean crossing. These MUST NOT be confused with No-Go Pills, which have the opposite effect. Pilots have mistakenly taken their No-Gos when they should have taken Gos, resulting in some interesting divert scenarios.

**Gouge** - Study material. If a fighter pilot must study and prepare for something, you can bet a gouge packet will be created in the process and passed on to the bros to help them when they have to cross the same bridge. It is one way a fighter pilot looks out for others.

**Hails and Farewells** - Social gatherings to welcome or bid farewell to members of the squadron. They are typically family-friendly events where both the military member and their spouse (if they have one) are honored.

**Heater** - Heat seeking missile. To Americans, this terms refers to the Aim-9.

**Hooch** - The living accommodations while TDY. Usually a hotel or base lodging.

**Hostile** - A contact meeting ROE may be declared hostile and can be fired upon. This term may also be used when referencing any of the pilot-haters on base who care less about the mission than they do about complicating your life.

**IFF** - Introduction to Fighter Fundamentals. Fighter pilots learn the basics of BFM during the few months they spend in IFF. If you can win a dogfight in a T-38, you can win one in *any* jet.

**IJ** - Instant Justice. The opportunity to call someone out at Roll Call thus getting the beef off the initiator's chest. Once an IJ is brought up, it is never spoken of again. It's instant, and it's just.

**IMC** - Instrument Meteorological Conditions. This is the weather that typically awaits you at home station when you return from a six-month deployment and have just flown a 10-hour sortie. It was previously hanging out in the tanker track making your rejoin with the tanker both exciting and painful.

**IPUG** - Instructor Pilot Upgrade. The upgrade all flight leads dread.

**Joker** - A pre-briefed fuel state that means it's time to move on to the next phase of the mission or you will not have enough gas to accomplish said phase.

**Keg Rule** - If you are the perpetrator of fratricide in a training scenario, you must buy a keg for the squadron of the pilot you accidentally "killed." You've felt the pain of committing fratricide in your heart. Now you must feel it in your wallet.

**Kissing Lieutenant** - Designated wingman in the squadron who is not married and who can perform kissing duties at squadron hails and farewells. Must make the right decision when the crowd is telling him to "kiss her on the lips" as he kisses the spouse of a bro at the end of the ceremony.

**Landing Fee** - When you first arrive in the squadron, you must pay an upfront fee to the LPA called a *landing fee*. The fee covers the mementos that will eventually be purchased and given to you when you leave the squadron. This fee is separate from your squadron dues and varies by squadron. Always complain about it; always pay it!

**LFE** - Large Force Exercise. These combat training missions involve numerous aircraft of different types. It is not out of the norm for one hundred aircraft or more to participate in the larger exercises. Red Flag is an example of an LFE.

**Limfac** - Short for *limiting factor*. This is something no fighter pilot wants to be. You didn't want to be the kid for whom the whole bus pulled over on the field trip because you had to take a leak. Don't be that guy or gal in the squadron who needs special consideration because you can't make it happen!

**LPA** - Lieutenant Protection Association. They have to get mutual support from somewhere; why not each other? The LPA is the unofficial organization of lieutenants in the squadron who help each other fulfill some of the less desirable duties in the squadron such as Snack-O.

**"M"-word** - Derogatory term for a Master's Degree. We didn't have beef with higher education until it was made a requirement for promotion. The requirement has since been rescinded, but we all hate the idea of having to earn an advanced degree while flying fighters full time.

**Mayor** - The social director of the squadron. Runs Roll Call.

**Mort** - Another name for a dead man or getting killed in an engagement. If you soaked up a valid shot from Red Air, you're a mort!

**MIL Power** - The maximum throttle setting a fighter pilot can set without the use of afterburner.

**MQT** - Mission Qualification Training. The last hurdle a young fighter pilot must pass before becoming a combat mission ready wingman (at least on paper.)

**Nickel on the Grass** - When a fighter pilot is done fighting in this world and departs for his next mission (i.e. morts), the bros will throw a nickel on the grass next to his grave. This tradition has two roots: 1) Greek myth tells of a need for a dead soul to pay a coin to the boatman as payment for passage across the River Styx, and 2) An old Salvation Army Song was modified from "Throw a nickel on the drum and you'll be saved," to "Throw a nickel on the grass and save a fighter pilot's ass." Fighter pilots have since clung to these words. A toast that is often given at the passing of a fighter pilot goes like this:

"So here's a nickel on the grass to you, my friend, and your spirit, enthusiasm, sacrifice and courage — but most of all to your friendship. Yours is a dying breed and when you are gone, the world will be a lesser place."

**No-Go Pills** - Sleep aids issued by the flight doc to help pilots adjust their sleep schedule. They are normally issued when the flying schedule switches from days (with 0630 takeoff times) to nights (which can involve takeoffs at all hours of the night.) If you are issued these before a pond crossing, put them in your packed bag and do not bring them in the cockpit with you!

**O'Club** - Officer's Club. This term is also starting to fade with time. Back when money was plentiful and budgets were merely a formality, there existed both an Officer's Club and an Enlisted Club. With today's cost restraints, many clubs have consolidated to a single building known simply as *the Club*. Historically, the O'Club was a haven for officers/pilots to let their hair down and relax in a safe environment. As such, it was a popular place to go and would be packed on any given weekend. Nowadays, many clubs are closing due to the lack of customers. Because of the increasing pressure for political correctness and the implementation of rules, fighter pilots have sought out establishments that are more friendly towards our behavior and not as risk averse as on-base clubs are.

**Pickle** - The action of pressing the pickle button — the button on the aircraft control stick that releases ordnance. This term is also used to describe the act of giving birth. For example: "My wife is scheduled to pickle next Friday night, so I'll have to go straight to the hospital from Roll Call."

**Piddle-Pack** - Also known as a pilot relief bag. The Piddle Pack is a fighter pilot's best friend on long sorties like ocean crossings. It is the only outhouse onboard a single-seat fighter. While sometimes tricky to use (especially if wearing a poopie suit—see below) it is worth the spillage and hassle. It is not uncommon for a pilot to use three or more on an ocean crossing. Just don't leave one in the jet or your crew chief will make sure you pay dearly. Oh, and no "number 2s" please...

**Poopie Suit** - No, this is not the companion to the Piddle Pack. This is simply a nickname for an anti-exposure suit. It's a dry suit made of rubber and worn over your undergarments. It is required to wear when flying over areas where the water temperature is less than 60 degrees Fahrenheit (can be waived to 50 degrees.) Again, no "number 2s" please, no matter what the older pilots in the squadron tell you.

**Profile** - All fighter jets have an optimal climb profile that is often referred to simply as *the profile*. This term is also used in the bar with similar connotations. When a pilot consumes several alcoholic beverages early in the night, they are considered to be on the profile.

**Punk** - A freshly minted wingman, usually a 2nd or 1st Lieutenant, and member of the LPA. Punks are the workhorses of the squadron and keep the rest of us young.

**Queep** - This is the second ugliest word in the fighter pilot's vocabulary. Queep is non-flying-related work such as writing a performance report or volunteering for a meaningless (to pilots) duty like being the project officer for a change of command ceremony. Queep cannot be avoided but must be accomplished efficiently. The second worst sin a fighter pilot can commit is putting off doing queep so that a bro must do it for him.

**RAF** - Royal Air Force. We typically refer to the Brits when using the term *RAF*, but many other air forces in the world use the title *Royal Air Force* in their name. Whether hanging out with the Brits (RAF), the Aussies (RAAF), or the Canadians (RCAF), you can plan on having an awesome time!

**Red Air** - The simulated bad guys in an air combat training scenario. No one volunteers to be Red Air, but most pilots gladly snatch up the assignment to be the villain.

**RMO** - Round Metal Object. You better not say "coin," or you're issuing a challenge. This is not a challenge, put your RMO back.

**ROE** - Rules of Engagement. Lawyers create them for combat, fighter pilots create them for the bar. Both require significant study. Both carry grave consequences if broken.

**RTB** - Return to Base. This term can be used while TDY when leaving the bar to go back to the hotel.

**SA** - Situational Awareness. You either have it, or you don't. If you have lost it, you probably don't know it until you get it back.

**Shack** - This word has two meanings. The first meaning is used to indicate ordnance has squarely hit its intended target. The second meaning is to be called out for committing a transgression of a squadron rule. For example, if you drove one of the few rental cars the squadron had on a TDY and took the keys flying with you while the bros on the ground needed transportation, you would be *shacked* and assessed a fine of some sort.

**Scribe** - The guy who documents your heinous acts at Roll Call and reads them back at the following Roll Call, so everyone remembers.

**Shoe Clerk** - A derogatory term used to refer to non-flying or non-tactical military members who could care less if the mission is a success or not. Periodically, the fighter pilot will need assistance from one of these individuals. What usually ends up happening is the Shoe Clerk tells the fighter pilot they are unable to help them, at which point the fighter pilot learns their job and does it for them because they are absolutely useless. It's like buying shoes—it saves time if the shoe clerk can find the right size for you, but you can eventually find the size yourself.

**Shoe Clerk 500** - A term used to describe the massive influx of traffic through the base gate at 0800 (the morning rush) and the outflow through the same gate at 1600 (the afternoon rush.) Usually not experienced by the fighter pilot who shows between 0500 and 0600 and doesn't leave until 1800 or later.

**Shotmeister** - The guy who pours the shots, so no one remembers what the Scribe just read.

**Slizzard** - A brevity term created in the 8ᵗʰ Fighter Squadron used to describe someone who intends to needlessly merge with an adversary without affecting mission outcome. In general, a pilot who is *Slizzard* probably lacked the awareness required to merge and ended up turning with the enemy. Had the pilot been more aware, he would have stiff-armed the enemy and gone home with the rest of his formation.

**Snack-O** - Short for "Snack Officer." The Snack-O is typically filled by a lieutenant wingman. The Snack-O is in charge of keeping the squadron snack bar stocked. The Snack-O will also raise money for the social fund by selling t-shirts, patches, and other squadron memorabilia. It is a money losing business endeavor and will forever be so.

**SNAP** - Sensitive New Age Pilot. This term refers to the young generation of fighter pilots who expect everything to be handed to them. They expect a pat on the back and a golden star regardless of the level of their performance. SNAPs spend an inordinate amount of time caring for their appearance and get upset if you debrief them for being out of position.

**So to Speak** - A term used following any word or phrase that could possibly have inappropriate connotations. It's a way to say what you want to say by not saying it, but saying something so you can say it. Also used are the terms *so to say, phrasing,* and *in a manner of speaking.*

**Sock Check** - This tradition has all but faded. Fighter squadrons used to issue their pilots a pair of socks embroidered with the squadron insignia. The socks would be worn to Roll Call and could be verified one time during the night by initiating a Sock Check. If someone yelled "SOCK CHECK!" each pilot would drop his/her flight suit down past their ankles revealing their socks (among other things.) It was a short-lived tradition that is not carried on today. It is funny, nonetheless.

**SOF** - Supervisor of Flying. The lonely job of sitting up in the control tower while the bros are flying. The SOF gets the bros back before the surprise thunderstorm rolls in, or forces them to divert to the nearest location with good weather and a golf course.

**Songbook** - (Also known as a hymnal) A book containing words to the favorite fighter pilot songs in the squadron. Can also contain other social rules of engagement specific to the squadron. Songbooks have largely vanished since the great Witch Hunt of 2012 when any material that could possibly be construed as offensive was ordered to be cleared from the squadron and destroyed.

**Songmeister** - The guy in charge of cueing the music at the direction of the Mayor. Also may be the instigator of songs at any time in the bar.

**SPINS** - Special Instructions. SPINS are provided by combatant commanders to those operating in their area of responsibility. They give guidance on how to fight given the current political situation and usually contain the theater ROE.

**TDY** - Temporary Duty (or Temporary Duty Yonder when people used to say *yonder*.) A fighter pilot's "work vacation." See the chapter on TDY.

**UPT** - Undergraduate Pilot Training. Often called JSUPT (Joint Specialized Undergraduate Pilot Training) or SUPT. UPT is where Air Force pilots receive initial flight training. Upon successful completion of UPT, they receive their wings.

**VFR** - Visual Flight Rules. Less restrictive than Instrument Flight Rules, therefore favored by fighter pilots everywhere except those near complicated airspaces like Washington DC.

**WATT** - Weapons and Tactics Talk. You're a better person for it.

**3-Letter "S"** - Reference to Squadron Officer School (aka "SOS" or "Shoe Flag.") This is a five- to eight-week course (depending upon the flavor of the year) that provides instruction on how to be an Air Force leader in the squadron organization. It is a necessary part of an Air Force officer's progression through the ranks, but that doesn't erase the fact that it takes away from flying! It is loathed by fighter pilots everywhere and is considered a naughty word.

**$5 Rule** - Sometimes the tactical situation looks different in the heat of battle than it does when you review the mission on the ground. If you claim a kill on adversary airborne only find out the kill was invalid because you incorrectly assessed the effect of your missile, you pay the bandit who kill-removed (left the fight thinking he was dead) $5 for his trouble. Mistakes aren't free.

# Acknowledgements

This book wouldn't have been possible without my beautiful wife and partner in crime, Darcey. Thank you for watching the kids while I spent hours living the traditions, researching them, and writing them down. More importantly, thanks for your understanding when I stayed out late on Friday nights with the bros at Roll Call. You're my rock!

To my first real fighter squadron commander, Bluto, thanks for teaching me what it means to be a fighter pilot. You, Vasco, Raz'n, Lager, Motley, Sputnik, Gordo, Mac, and Bandit were the perfect group of bros to indoctrinate Splash and me into the brotherhood. You provided the exact right amount of "fear, sarcasm, and ridicule" to push me to be a better fighter pilot. You looked out for me unlike anyone else. I will ALWAYS be a Black Sheep!

Karlene Petitt, Eric "Cap'n Aux" Auxier, Mark Berry, Leland Shanle, Brent Owens, and Ron Rapp— thanks for letting me into the gang and helping me get motivated to write! Mark, Leland, and Karlene, thank you for your words of advice and for not pulling punches; you are helping me be a better writer.

I'd like to send a special thanks to my family of proofreaders. Mom, Dad, Rick, Steph and, of course, Darcey. You guys came through for me right at the end when I dropped the last-minute tasking on you. Thank you, thank you, thank you!

Finally, I'd like to recognize my parents. You helped me struggle through college and didn't even flinch when I told you I was throwing away a finance degree to go fly fast jets. You're the best!

# About the Author

Rob Burgon lives in Utah with his wife, Darcey, and their three budding fighter pilots: Everett, Layla, and Natalia. Rob spent nearly twelve years as an active duty pilot with the United States Air Force. He is a combat-experienced fighter pilot with over 2,000 hours of turbine engine time logged in the T-37, T-38, F-16, and F-22. Rob has now transitioned to commercial flying with a major U.S. airline, but still gets his fix flying fast jets with the United States Air Force Reserve.

Rob is the co-host of the *Slipstream Radio* Podcast and editor of Tally One (www.TallyOne.com), a military aviation blog. Rob has been featured in *There I Wuz Vol 3,* a popular aviation book series produced by Eric Auxier, and has appeared on the highly-regarded aviation podcasts *The Airplane Geeks* and *AviatorCast.* He is currently working on several fiction and non-fiction books, which he hopes to publish soon.

Made in the USA
Monee, IL
14 January 2021